GOOD
BUSINESS

by

Sheena Carmichael
&
John Drummond

Good Business

A Guide to Corporate Responsibility and Business Ethics

Sheena Carmichael and John Drummond

Business Books

Copyright © Sheena Carmichael and John Drummond 1989

First published in Great Britain by
Business Books Limited
An imprint of Century Hutchinson Limited
62-65 Chandos Place, London, WC2N 4NW

Century Hutchinson Australia (Pty) Limited
89-91 Albion Street, Surrey Hills,
New South Wales 2010, Australia

Century Hutchinson New Zealand Limited
PO Box 40-086, 32-34 View Road, Glenfield,
Auckland 10, New Zealand

Century Hutchinson South Africa (Pty) Limited
PO Box 337, Bergvlei 2012, South Africa

British Library Cataloguing in Publication Data
Carmichael, Sheena
  Good business: a guide to corporate
  responsibility and business ethics
  1. Business enterprise. Ethical aspects
  I. Title II. Drummond, John
  174'.4

  ISBN 0-09-174028-2
  ISBN 0-09-173949-7 Pbk

Phototypeset by Saxon Ltd, Derby
Printed and bound in Great Britain by
Mackays of Chatham PLC, Chatham, Kent

ACKNOWLEDGMENTS

We owe a real and lasting debt to Kay Carmichael, who conceived the outline of the book and told us to get on with it, and to Bryan Janson-Smith and Edward Posey, two experts in networking who made the connections for us.

Before that, it began with Ron Speed, initiator of the world's first One Per Cent Club, who fired John's imagination and kept his sense of humour through all the dumb questions.

We salute the memory of Harry Chapin, songwriter extraordinaire, who like us, believed in people, and of Leslie Forrester, an MD who believed in corporate responsibility.

For the Business Ethics section we have drawn heavily, with his permission, on the model of Dr Mark Pastin, Director of the Lincoln Center for Ethics at Arizona State University. Mark is perhaps the first academic to come at ethics from the point of view of the businessperson, rather than the philosopher or theologian; we are building on his foundations in our own work in the field.

ABOUT THE AUTHORS

SHEENA CARMICHAEL is Managing Director of Action for Corporate Responsibility. She trained as a journalist with the Thompson Organisation. Her first degree is in Politics and European Studies from Sussex University, and she also has a Master's in Tourism from Strathclyde Business School.

Her business experience comes from the travel trade, as Operations Director of an incoming tour operator and then running her own company which sold Italian tours to the American market. Her interest in an ethical approach to decision-making grew throughout ten years' service to the community as a magistrate and member of a Children's Panel.

JOHN DRUMMOND's background is in marketing and communications. He has a degree in electronics from Heriot Watt University and is also a Fellow of the British Institute of Management, Member of the Institute of Marketing, and a Member of the Institute of Public Relations.

His expertise in corporate responsibility developed in his role as communications executive for IBM, and then as Director of Communications for Honeywell. As Public Affairs Director of TSB during its highly successful flotation he managed a major public relations campaign.

John Drummond is also managing director of Communication Works, a successful London-based consultancy which advises organizations and individuals on all aspects of communications.

CONTENTS

PART I CORPORATE RESPONSIBILITY

PART III COMMUNICATION

PREFACE

This is the first British book in the field of corporate responsibility and business ethics that has been written expressly for the business person who does not have time to plough through complex philosophical justifications. Until now this debate has been the preserve of theologians and academics – business people have been too busy running their companies to participate.

Articles dealing with aspects of the subject appear with increasing frequency in management journals and newspapers. Awareness has been raised considerably by organizations like Business in the Community. Now it is time to gather together the best of current practice, and to look to the future.

As well as advancing some revolutionary concepts, this book seeks to be a guide for those who simply want to work more effectively in community relations, and sets out to explain ways in which that effectiveness can be improved. There are no other 'how to' books available to business people and others in this country with an interest in the subject.

The book is divided into three sections. They don't operate in a straight line – it's more of a sandwich effect. On either side of the sandwich are 'how to' guides which look at topics you are probably familiar with – topics which in most organizations come under the heads of marketing, human resources and public affairs.

The first discusses the issue of corporate responsibility. It can stand alone, as a straightforward guide which will enable you to take money which your organization is probably already spending and deploy it to greater effect. It is an exercise in simple economics.

We then extend the discussion to explain why business ethics are at the core of any corporate responsibility strategy. This is what we see as the 'meat' in our sandwich.

On the other side is our guide to communicating your strategy. It is vital that a commitment to an ethical or corporate responsibility approach should be communicated effectively, in order to gain the commitment in turn of all the stakeholder groups to that sense of corporate purpose.

We have tried very hard to avoid using jargon – either philosophical jargon or management jargon. We do not believe that sophisticated language is necessary to explain sophisticated concepts.

The concepts in this book are extremely sophisticated. But it is a book which can be probed to different depths. One reader may simply take three or four good ideas from the examples of best practice. He might decide to buy jerseys for the local football team, or to invite a sixth-former to 'shadow' him at work for a week.

Another reader may prefer to dwell on our analysis of the future development of organizational life, and project how his or her company is equipped to meet the moral and societal challenges of the twenty-first century.

We hope this book will be of as much value to the individual junior employee as to the managing director of a billion-pound company. If you are a managing director, we hope that having read this you will give copies to all your managers. It will also be helpful to community organizations looking for ways to interface with business.

We have recognized current reality to the extent that in general we refer to senior managers as 'he': our spelling checker throws back 'businesswoman' as an unrecognizable term, but we sincerely hope that by the time we write our next book enough of our advice will have been implemented to enable us to use both genders interchangeably.

PART I

Corporate Responsibility

CHAPTER ONE

ARE YOU PROUD TO SAY YOU'RE IN BUSINESS?

BUSINESS PEOPLE HAVE had a bad press since the days when newspapers were written on papyrus. Jesus threw the moneylenders out of the Temple. Three centuries earlier, Aristotle had hit the headlines, attacking merchants as 'parasites' totally lacking in virtue and social sense, who produced nothing of value. Shakespeare's Merchant of Venice shows clearly what they thought about businessmen in Elizabethan times. They weren't just unpopular, they were outcasts.

The world's first major business, in the modern sense, was the East India Company. Most of its managers were men who could not make a living at home in the professions, in the traditional way, or younger sons who would not inherit 'respectable' money. Not a few were the black sheep of their family. Novels of the period are full of discussions of the dilemma of young women from respectable families when the nabobs came home from India with all their money to find a wife – was the money worth the social disgrace of marrying a merchant?

Things aren't a lot better today. From *Open All Hours* to *Dallas* and *Dynasty*, people in business are still being portrayed as crooks. The little man in the corner shop holds down the scales to give his customers short weight. The boss of an oil company hires mercenaries to blow up an installation to give himself a competitive advantage. Two chief executives devote a large part of their business lives to trying to put each other out of business.

A study by the Media Institute in Washington found that two out of every three businessmen on television came across as foolish, greedy or downright evil. Almost half of all business activities were on the grey side of the law. And as few as three per cent of business people were portrayed as behaving in ways that benefit society.

There was once a programme on British television which showed a successful business person who tried to run an honest company. Even worse, it dealt with a woman running a building company. And worst of all, she had a good relationship with her young boyfriend. Even though the lead was played by Penelope Keith, the programme only ran for one series.

There is a big social gap between business people and others. Academics and professional people tend to mix with their own kind, and many of them do not happen to have any friends who are in business. Journalists and television producers and presenters usually see themselves on the academic/professional side of the divide, and they are the ones who decide the image of business which is put across in the media. It is easy to get the wrong idea about something if you don't really know much about it.

Businessmen are not bogeymen

There are some businessmen who don't do much to dispel the general impression that businessmen are baddies. When the chairman of Guinness makes a public promise to move his headquarters to Edinburgh and then, with the support of his board, pulls out of his obligation, the man in the street shrugs his shoulders and asks, what do you expect of businessmen? The thousands of people who had invested the money that was going to make their old age comfortable in Barlow Clowes must have a tiny suspicion somewhere that they were fools ever to trust a businessman – any businessman.

The motto of Harvard Business School is 'To Make Business a Profession'. Professions are distinguished by having certain standards or codes of conduct which all the members agree to follow. The penalty for not doing so is losing membership of that profession. Professionals such as doctors and lawyers are usually proud of their profession. But business is just as important to the fabric of our modern day society as legal services or medicine. Business is where the wealth is created, business gives people jobs, business pays taxes to fund our social services.

If businessmen want to be as proud of their work as doctors or lawyers they must be prepared to pay the price. They must act as responsibly as any professional. Many already do so to the limits of their ability. But while individuals can do a great deal even within their own little section of a large company – and we shall show later in the book how big an impact they can have – the burden of showing that business is responsible has to be carried by companies. The next question is:

Are you proud of your company?

Legally, a company is the shareholders and directors. But everyone knows that a company is more than that: it is also everyone who works for it. They are not the only people who have to be considered, though, when you are thinking about your company and the way it behaves.

A great many people have a stake in any company: customers, suppliers, former employees with company pensions, students who may be seeking work, and the community at large. This idea of the community at large is an important one, and it is a theme we shall be coming back to again and again. Why does it matter so much?

Companies are a relatively new phenomenon. Business has been carried on in some form or other throughout human history. But the limited company – the corporation – has only existed for a couple of hundred years. We tend to assume that this is the only way of ordering society, and so it is bound to continue. But it isn't. Can you be sure that there will still be business and companies, in the sense we know, today, in a hundred years' time? *We* can't. But if there is a consensus that this is a good way to structure our economic life, we need to look at what allows a business to survive.

Obviously it must be profitable. But no matter how good a product, how big the market, it requires one extra thing – the society in which it operates must permit it to exist.

Take cigarettes. If society were to decide that it was no longer prepared to pay the human cost of allowing the manufacture of tobacco products, tobacco companies would cease to exist. (Awareness of this is already causing them to diversify at a rate of knots.) On a smaller scale, if a small shopkeeper is convicted of giving short measure and defrauding customers over a period of years, the community in which his shop is located is likely to decide that it is not going to buy from him any more.

Of the ten largest companies operating in the UK, US and Germany before the First World War, eight no longer exist. We believe that one of the reasons for this is that they lost the confidence of the communities in which they were operating.

Society is changing. If companies want to survive these changes, they need to change themselves in a way which is acceptable to society. And if the people who work for a company feel proud of it, that's a pretty accurate indicator of whether it mirrors the values of the rest of the community.

If you answered yes to our first two questions, about feeling proud to say you're a businessman and feeling proud of your company, our next question may not apply to you. For those of you – and you're probably the majority – who couldn't give a wholehearted 'yes', we ask:

Do you want to feel good about yourself?

We all want to feel good. And one of the quickest ways to stop feeling good is for one part of you to be doing things of which another part doesn't approve.

You know the feeling. You've just been on the phone to an irate customer, swearing blind to them that it must be the courier service which has delayed the order, when you know it was the mix-up in your own stockroom. Or you've persuaded the owner of a small, struggling business to buy a new piece of office equipment outright when it would have been better for him to lease it, because you've made your month's target on leasing but not on sales.

You use the office photocopier to copy a private letter. Nobody has problems with that, surely? But the next day is Saturday, and you come in to run off three hundred copies of your club's newsletter. Maybe you feel a little uneasy about that one.

We can all think of things we do every day which, if we really sat down and thought about them, would make us uneasy. And the reason they would make us feel that way is that deep down we know them to be wrong.

'Holism' has become a fashionable concept. The Prince of Wales talks about holistic medicine. Local authorities talk about holistic approaches to the problem of the inner cities. Holism means taking the *whole* picture into account. In this case, it means accepting that the kind of person you are at home with your family is the same kind of person you are at work. You may feel the need to *behave* differently – we all know that there is a way to do things at work, and if you don't do it that way you may lose your job – but you are the same person underneath.

There *is* one way to feel good about what you do. That is to bring both parts of you into line. Act in business the way you would act towards the family and friends you care about. Act ethically.

Ethics is a loaded word. Business ethics? You've got to be joking, say the cynics, it's a contradiction in terms. But ethical simply means moral, and to be moral means to do right. Businesses are made up of people. **If people want to be good, and people want to do right, then business can, and will, be ethical.**

No man is an island

John Donne said it over three hundred years ago, and it's even more true today.

Aerosol sprays containing CFCs are being phased out in the UK because they damage the ozone layer. Citizens of the United States are beginning to realize that they need the South American rain forests if they want to go on breathing good air. There is nowhere left where you can have sex with a stranger and be confident you won't catch Aids.

A company's market used to be its local area. Now trans-national companies see their market as worldwide. The single European market is the subject of a major UK government publicity campaign.

Interdependence used to mean that a man depended on his family and friends, his small local community. Now if he is a car worker in Sunderland, he may depend on a design engineer in Japan to produce car designs which will sell in this country and keep him in his job. His wife might run a business importing knitting yarns from France, which in turn she uses to produce knitwear which finds a market in the United States. Their son might have a disease which is kept under control by a drug discovered in New Zealand; their daughter may process computer data originating in Canada.

In business, new ways of working are being developed which will depend much more on people being able to trust each other, and realize that they are in fact interdependent.

We shall be discussing the concept of the Lean, or hollowed out, Organization, which is the way many companies are moving. Head office staff are trimmed to the minimum, and all those functions which can be moved are devolved to consultants, former employees and others who specialize in a particular area.

The importance of this is that a much greater degree of trust will be needed, and fair play will be expected. But, as anyone in business knows, you cannot rely on others to be as fair with you as you are with them – unless their company is quite clear about its position. Because nobody wants to put their job in danger by going against what is seen as the proper way to behave.

Caring is not just altruism

The other main consequence of growing interdependence is that the days have gone when we could make short-term decisions without thinking of their long-term results. It is particularly difficult for business people to think in the long term. Half-yearly results are not enough any more – the financial analysts who determine share prices are looking at quarterly results. One set of bad figures and institutions withdraw their support. Even when a company sets out with a declared intention of looking to the long term, as did Virgin, the market reacts on a short-term basis.

In the Middle Ages great cathedrals were built all over Europe. The workmen who toiled on the foundations knew that they would be dead long before it was completed – 150 years from start to finish was not uncommon. But they knew that what they were building would endure, and enrich their community for many generations to come.

We are not suggesting that businesses should plan for a century from now – though the ICIs and General Motors may well be. What we are saying is that, looking five or ten years ahead, the most important variable in the success of your business will be the way it is regarded by the community in which it operates.

Every time you go out and buy something you are making a choice, and that choice is becoming more informed. For instance, consumers have voted not to accept the penalties of drinking too much alcohol – so low alcohol products are being developed to fill the gap. Caring about the issues which affect all of us is basic market research.

We shall be looking at how much it costs *not* to care, and at the same time demonstrating how easy it is to care, with many cost-effective ways of improving performance. We have heard so often how you'd like to do things differently, but.... **It** *can* **be done. Everyone in business wants to feel good, and everyone wants to be part of a successful business. There is a way, and it involves going down the road of corporate responsibility – the ethical road.**

CHAPTER TWO

CAN BUSINESSES BE GOOD CITIZENS TOO?

CORPORATE RESPONSIBILITY IS a high-faluting term for describing the attitude of a business which wants to be the kind of good citizen you want to be in your private life. You need food and shelter to survive; the business needs to make profits to survive.

Those are the basics. But for long-lasting successful survival we need a lot more. Babies deprived of physical contact, though fed and kept warm, do not grow properly. They are ill more often, and they grow up as incomplete people unable to have warm, loving relationships with others. And that in turn means they are much less productive than they might otherwise have been.

A responsible business accepts, of course, that its first job is to make sure it survives. But just as there are many things in life other than food and shelter that you need to survive successfully, the responsible business needs to look beyond just making profits.

While companies are a relatively new entity, businesses have been around for ever. What is the difference?

What changed was that the owners of businesses stopped being the people who *ran* the business. They started to employ managers, instead of managing things themselves. Before this, even where owners had devolved most of the day-to-day running to managers, they had still felt a personal involvement and were always a final court of appeal in disputes.

Many different groups have a part to play in the success of a company: these groups are frequently called *stakeholders*.

Employees are stakeholders. So are shareholders, directors, customers, suppliers, and the community at large.

Later when we give you the tools to solve ethical problems in business, the starting point will be to identify all the stakeholders involved in any particular decision. The more viewpoints you take into account, the more likely you are to find the right answer.

So the greatest change when businesses turned themselves into limited companies was that decisions stopped being made by people who were part of two stakeholder groups (owners and managers) and started being made by just one group, managers. It is a matter of common sense that a manager who might change his job next week or next year will look at things differently from an owner who wants his children to take over his business in thirty years' time.

Many of the notable social advances in Victorian times came from businessmen who saw what they were doing as part of their civic duty. When Robert Owen built his mills at New Lanark he considered every aspect of his workers' welfare. The great Quaker chocolate-making families cared for their workforce in ways that other employers found hard to understand – and they did it simply because they thought it was the right and ethical thing to do.

This way of behaving can be dismissed as paternalism, and it probably would not work today. But the important point is that although these things were done for ethical reasons, they also did a lot to contribute to the success of the companies. There are no mills at New Lanark now because new technology has taken over. Rowntree Mackintosh (despite its recently acquired Swiss parent) and Cadbury, however, are two of the oldest-established companies in the United Kingdom.

But as a business is made up of people, if an individual can be a good citizen, so too can a business. Marks and Spencer have always believed that the wealth of the high street depends on the health of the back street. From their earliest days they have worked to make sure that they do what they can to help. The Body Shop, Company of the Year in 1988, insists that all its shops have a project in the local area – such as the sales staff doing free facials in an old people's home.

It is not enough, though, to leave this to chance. Only through budgeting can we buy the things we really want. For a business to act as a good citizen it needs to think through the best ways to do it – to have a *structure* and a *strategy*. We deal with these step-by-step in the second half of the book.

What is it going to cost?

It's a cold, hard world out there. Your competitors are waiting to take your markets. How can you agree to put any of your profits towards charity, when you need to plough the money back into the business? Why should you waste good money on allowing employees time off to run the local boys' club, when you need them here, producing *real* income? And as for bringing a yoga teacher into the factory in company time, do we have any idea what that would do to productivity?

Well, yes, actually. It would probably *increase* it. So would the other things mentioned above. Costs can be looked at in two ways. What it costs to do something – and what it costs *not* to do it.

Some companies with headquarters in Minneapolis believe 5% of gross profit is the right figure. That is the amount they are prepared to put into corporate responsibility, into being good citizens. And these are not corner shops – they are some of the leading names in the Fortune 500. They believe it would cost them a lot more *not* to contribute.

In the UK companies are more cautious. The largest single commitment is generally 1%. In addition, many large companies have joined the Per Cent Club, usually giving half a per cent. But the level of financial commitment is not the important factor – it is the acceptance of the principle that this is something your company needs to do to be successful.

We find that the majority of British companies are actually doing quite a lot in terms of what we would call corporate responsibility. But because the approach is often unsystematic, without a clear policy at senior management level, they do not always do it in the most cost-effective way.

It is not uncommon to encounter *'The Chairman's Secretary Syndrome'*. You've seen it in action. A local group writes to a company asking if they have any old typewriters they could donate. The boys' club writes asking for a contribution to buying football strips. The local hospital is trying to endow a new ward, and offers to name it after the company. A refuge for battered women needs a new carpet, and would love your cast-offs.

Where do these letters end up? Sometimes in the personnel department. Sometimes with the finance director. But more often than not nobody is quite sure who deals with these issues, and they end up on the desk of the Chairman. He asks his secretary to sift them and tell him which ones she thinks are the most deserving.

The secretary may – probably does – know more about the company than many senior managers. She may know the size of the budget the Chairman privately allocates to 'good works'. **But it is highly unlikely that she is making decisions in response to a corporate strategy which has decided the priority areas for giving and quantified the likely payback in each area.**

It is sometimes a revelation to companies when they sit down and measure how much they are already spending on corporate responsibility. In particular, companies with a relatively small HQ and a large number of branch operations can find they are contributing significantly to the local communities in which they operate.

Obviously, detailed decisions have to be made at local level, where community needs become clear, and where they need to be met. But you wouldn't make any other major investment decisions without a clear strategy, and this could be one of the most vital such decisions you ever make.

Of course you don't *have* to do anything: lots of companies don't. But we would argue that the cost to those companies is very heavy indeed. It will be a lot greater than any saving to be made through not spending money for the benefit of *all* the stakeholders.

We know there is going to be a severe shortage of skilled workers in the next decade. People who have values in their own life which go further than just making money are likely to want to work for companies which feel the same way. So difficulty in recruitment is one of the major costs to a company which does not invest in responsibility.

Retention is another factor. Finding the right employee is only half the solution – keeping him or her is the other. Losing staff in whom they have invested a lot of time and money is a heavy cost for some companies. And any good manager will tell you that just raising salaries is not the answer.

There is also the cost in lost sales. Other things being equal, customers will choose to shop at the store with a reputation for fair dealing. One of the most important factors in Marks and Spencer's phenomenally high sales rates per square foot is its policy of unquestioningly giving refunds on unsuitable goods. Customers will take a chance on an impulse purchase knowing that they *can* change their minds. They probably won't, and the sale is made.

Lack of customer loyalty is another cost. Repeat business is the best business. Customers are more likely to know their requirements, with a consequent saving of your sales staff's time. They have already shown they are credit-worthy, so your accounts department wastes less time chasing them up. They will recommend you to their friends and colleagues. How many of us are desperate for reliability and honest dealing above all, be it the services of a window cleaner or a mainframe computer we are shopping for?

Perhaps the biggest cost of all in not behaving responsibly is the risk of government intervention. It was because some traders were giving short weight that the Weights and Measures Acts were passed. Some companies ducked their responsibilities when the goods they supplied proved faulty – so the Sale of Goods Act went on the statute books. Now the Prime Minister is signalling her concern about the environment – a clear warning to companies that unless they clean up their act and curtail pollution there could be further legislation to force them to do it.

All of these costs can cripple a business. And unethical behaviour within a business can do more than all the rest put together to subtract from the bottom line.

There are a few companies who disregard all this. The ones out for a quick buck, the fly boys who plan to make a quick killing and disappear to Gibraltar or South America.

At the other end of the spectrum are companies with a structure, policy and programme in place to implement a strategy of corporate responsibility. Not many, but a growing number. If you work for one of them, you will know it and feel good about it. We hope this book helps you understand *why* it works.

But in the middle lies the vast majority of British companies. Companies who *do* see themselves as responsible, who *do* contribute to the community in one way or another. Managers in such companies often tell us: 'I'd love to do more, but I don't have the resources.'

Do you think being responsible costs too much?

It is surprising how often it costs nothing at all. In his concept of lateral thinking, Edward de Bono suggested that a tough problem could often be solved by thinking about it in a different way: sideways, rather than in a straight line.

That is what we propose. The starting point is the same as for ethical decision-making – taking the interests of *all* the stakeholders into account. Here are a couple of examples.

Not many people realize that companies often receive the greatest loyalty from employees who have just retired. Loyalty is one of a company's greatest resources, and there should be a way to capitalize on it. Most communities have voluntary groups needing the sort of skills your retired employees possess: plumbers, accountants, secretaries, managers – they can all be put to good use.

Men and women who have just retired don't want to be put out to grass. They want to feel useful, and to contribute. They may no longer wish to work forty hours a week: they have their pension, and money may no longer be the motivator. They would like to go on having some of the social contact they had at work; and to go on having their skills recognized: *they want to feel good about themselves.*

If your company acts as broker to bring these two groups together, what will it cost? Provision of an office, typewriter and a phone, perhaps, on a part-time basis, and maybe a little help from a secretary to run the database. **The investment is almost nothing. But consider the rewards:**

- The community benefits from expertise it could not afford to buy. Projects which might otherwise fail get off the ground or keep running.
- The retired people benefit. They feel good about themselves.
- The company benefits. It gets a name both as a good employer which sees its obligation to its workers as continuing past retirement, and as a caring member of the local community. That's the kind of company people want to work for and buy from.

Even a fairly small company could easily do this. But lateral thinking can work on the grand scale, too, to look at some of the major problems in society today.

Inner city issues are high on everyone's agenda. Honeywell, a large company based in Minneapolis, was outgrowing its headquarters building. It was located in the inner city, in an area of derelict housing with few of the amenities workers wanted around them. Quite frankly, it wasn't a nice place to work.

The straight line solution was simple: to do what everyone else does, and relocate to the leafy green suburbs. Nobody ever lost his job for recommending a safe solution, guaranteed to work. But Honeywell made a different choice.

They elected to stay and extend the existing building. The money that they saved in this way they spent for the benefit of the local community. They formed a partnership with the local authority, and helped to build houses, improve transport, and landscape open spaces. The local authority opened an art gallery. Shops moved in. What they ended up with was an inner city which was a good place to live *and* work in, offices which met their needs, and a first-rate reputation in the local community. And it all cost no more than the move to the suburbs would have done. *That's* lateral thinking.

CHAPTER THREE

WHY SHOULD A COMPANY BE RESPONSIBLE?

CHANGES IN POPULATION over the next five to fifteen years are going to have an enormous effect on business. For many years now, the number of people retiring has been roughly balanced by the number of young entrants to the workforce from schools and colleges. But between 1964 and 1977, the number of children born in the UK dropped from 1,015,000 to just 657,000: that is, by more than a third.

All the people you are going to recruit to your company by the year 2000 have already been born. Smart employers are already thinking of ways round the shortage – and those who wait too long to work out their strategy will be behind in the race.

In 1988 the Norwich Union Insurance Company made an offer of employment to every single school and college leaver in the Norwich area who met their basic entry requirements. What happened to all the other local employers who needed new recruits?

By the early 1990s the National Health Service will need at least *one in three of all female school leavers* with 5 'O' level equivalents or better to train as nurses, if the present level of supply is to be kept up. This is an impossible target. What is the Department of Health's answer? An advertising campaign aimed at school leavers.

The NHS has a huge reservoir of highly trained nurses. They leave the profession in droves every year, and not simply because of the strains of the job, or the low pay. They leave because nursing is incompatible with their family commitments. *Yet again, money is not the only motivator.* In a recent National

Economic Development Office report a pharmaceutical company says, 'It was like finding a hidden reserve of people when we altered shift patterns to attract women returners. Our old excuses for not employing returners – the hassle, turnover, kids – became pretty thin. It's an embarrassment that we have taken this long to adapt.'

By 1995, the UK workforce is predicted to increase by 800,000. 83% of this number will be women: four out of five new employees. Women have always instinctively understood holism better than men – they are the ones who have had to juggle the priorities.

With all the advances in equal opportunities, and even though men are helping out more, women are still the ones sorting out the children and the housework *and* looking after their husbands. Their job is just one factor which has to be balanced with the rest.

Women have different priorities from men: not superwomen, but ordinary women – the vast bulk of the female workforce in this country. An experiment in north London which increased the level of street lighting for a trial period had interesting results. Fewer than half the men questioned had even noticed the improvement. Almost all the women had. Fewer than one man in five thought it was a good idea – four out of five women welcomed it.

Here was an issue that mattered to women, and men did not even see it as a problem. There are lots of other issues that matter to women which business has not until now needed to bother about. But if they matter to 83% of new additions to the workforce, then it will be a foolish company which does not take them seriously.

Women are not the only reservoir of new workers, of course. The US Department of Labor predicts that by the year 2000, four out of five new company employees will be women, members of minorities or immigrants.

Some companies are already thinking laterally – those who have already been hit by the shortages. Tesco are taking on older workers in the area inside the M25. Sainsbury's search for new sources of labour in London led them to advertise in ethnic minority newspapers and magazines, and to offer special training to those who didn't meet their normal requirements. Sixty per cent of the new trainees were Afro-Caribbean. One Sainsbury store manager said it was important for the company to establish a reputation in the area as a responsible employer. But it was also a commercial decision: the company needed to turn to the long-term unemployed as an alternative source of staff.

Is your company working out its personnel strategies for the next decade? Does it realize that commercial decisions and social responsibility go hand in hand? In order to fulfil its commercial need for new people, it will need to ask: *Why do people work?*

We shall look into that question from the point of view of the individual in the next section. Now we shall examine it from the point of view of the company. What sort of things can the company offer which employees will value, in a situation where skilled workers can pick and choose?

Charles Handy, whose book *The Future of Work* published in 1984 has already proved remarkably accurate in many of its predictions, believes that training will be one of the key factors: 'Training is still regarded by many employers as a kind of punishment. You are sent on a course if you are not quite up to the mark. But if the up-to-dateness of your skills is one of the things that principally determines your earning power, training becomes a key component in the reward structure.'

Training is not a punishment – or even a reward. Training is a vital part of company survival strategy. It is not only the absolute decline in numbers of school leavers that is a problem: it is also the decline in the number of people trained in specific skills. Between 1985 and 1987 the number of applications for university places in physics fell by 12%, in engineering and technology by 11% and in maths by 9%.

One of the main things that stops companies investing in training is the fear that other companies will poach their skilled workers from them. **Poaching is an ethical issue. A company**

**that has a policy which says that poaching is wrong is one
which is likely to be trying to bring its values into line with the
values of its employees. It is also the company the best people
will want to work for.**

There are many inducements companies can offer staff: high
salaries, mortgage subsidies, company cars. But the problem is
that every other company can offer these too. The key is not to
be found in cash terms: it is to be found in a responsible attitude.

If good people are a company's most valuable asset, the loyalty
of those people is beyond price. And in a business environment
where mergers and takeovers proliferate – especially hostile
takeovers – a loyal workforce could mean the difference
between winning and losing.

What are the roots of motivation?

The Taylor Nelson company has been doing research for many
years on what matters to people – on the way they look at life.
They divide society into three groups: the sustenance-driven,
the outer-directed and the inner-directed:

Sustenance-driven people want to keep things as they are.
They don't care about much outside their family and their
home.

Outer-directed people want to be somewhere else. They want
more – more money, more status, more things.

The inner-directed have moved a stage further. They care
about the wider issues. They are not too keen on accepting
authority without question. Most change in our society comes
from the inner-directed – the Green movement is a good
example.

This is a developmental model, which means that people start
in the sustenance stage and, as their life circumstances change
and grow, make their way through to the other two stages. Not
everybody does, of course: many people spend their life very
happily in one of the first two stages.

**The findings of the Taylor Nelson research, carried out in
many countries over many years, are clear. More and more**

people are moving into the group they call inner directed. Currently in the UK about 36% of adults are in that category.

What does this mean for your company? It means that a growing part of your workforce is looking beyond the traditional rewards which you offer. *Shared values are the motivator of the future.*

Unemployment

Some companies do not have problems of recruitment or retention. Perhaps they have long-established links with sources of new well-trained staff, and think they know how to keep them. What are the advantages of responsibility for them?

Nobody likes unemployment. Even companies which benefit from a large reserve of unemployed workers would probably prefer to be operating within a healthy growing economy. The majority of the efforts of companies in the UK who try to become involved in the community are probably directed towards this one problem, through initiatives such as Enterprise Trusts.

But unemployment also *costs*. It costs business an enormous amount, in both direct and hidden costs. The direct costs are straightforward: the higher taxes everyone, including business, has to pay to support the social security system. Nearly one third of taxes paid to the Inland Revenue comes directly from companies in the form of Corporation Tax. And it is not only unemployment benefit that has to be paid for. The north/south divide in health is largely a result of the difference between being in work and out of work. Unemployed people visit the doctor more often, take up more hospital beds, need more prescriptions than people in work. Lack of work is a contributory factor to family breakdown. This costs more in support from the social services.

Families living on the dole are effectively living outside the major part of the consumer market. They don't buy new clothes. They don't buy new shoes – except maybe for the children.

They don't buy newspapers, magazines, birthday cards, holidays, hairdos, sports gear, home computers, crystal glasses, dishwashers, freezers, new furniture, restaurant meals..... they don't buy nine tenths of the products business is out there trying to sell.

One thing unemployed people do share with the rest of us, however, is television. This shows all the consumer goods the rest of us take for granted: goods which the long-term unemployed feel they will never have a chance to come by honestly – so some, *not many, but some*, choose to go out and take them dishonestly. The man or woman with a steady job on trial for theft in a magistrate's court is the exception, not the rule.

Shoplifting is not the only theft problem for retailers. Shrinkage is even worse: internal theft costs, too. Shrinkage happens when employees convince themselves that taking something won't hurt. Few shop assistants, office workers or factory employees would see themselves as criminal. This is an ethical issue – if the worker does not see his company as behaving responsibly, why should he himself behave responsibly?

Responsibility and ethics are all bound up together. The world of business, as portrayed on television is one of villains who take, take, take. If a company does not take positive steps to project a different image, its employees will not see themselves as criminal – maybe just as getting their own back. And of course projecting the image alone is not enough: reality has to match the image.

The drug problem is another aspect of the same issue. Many boys and girls living in inner city slums or desolate peripheral housing estates feel they are not part of society: they're not going to lead the lives of the families they see on television. They do not share the values of the rest of society. They're the ones who fall prey to the heroin dealers.

The most widespread drug of all is alcohol. The cost to business cannot be fully quantified, but runs to hundreds of millions of pounds a year, not just in days lost through absenteeism but also in deals lost through impaired performance, bungled decisions, loss of respect.

Health in general is an area where the returns on behaving responsibly are enormous. Traditionally health education in the workplace has been seen in terms of accident prevention and protection from dangerous machinery and substances. Many employers, while meeting the basic requirements laid down by the Health and Safety at Work Act, do not take account of how an employee's physical and psychological health might affect the ability to perform effectively.

American health-care company Ethicon, who started their Live for Life project in 1983, rate their absenteeism level at almost nil. Later on we will describe ways for *your* company to achieve that sort of figure.

Business can ignore all this, but everyone should be doing the sums. Either you encourage employees to behave ethically or you spend more millions every year on security. Either you encourage your workforce to live a healthy lifestyle, or you count the costs of high absenteeism.

As long as society has these problems, the costs have to be paid. Business can leave it to government to deal with them, or it can start to tackle them itself. Either way, it costs.

Governments, however, tend to respond to issues as they arise. But the best business people know that prevention is better than cure, and the ones who stay on top are those who feel they can influence events, who welcome and even demand change.

CHAPTER FOUR

WHY SHOULD YOU BE RESPONSIBLE?

IT IS VERY EASY to opt out. In business, you see all round you people behaving – not to mince words – dishonestly. You read that the Institute of Directors estimates rip-offs at £3.3 billion, that is £14 million in white-collar fraud every working day of the year. You're doing very nicely, thank you. You'd never dream of *evading* your taxes, though you'll do what you can to *avoid* them. And as for the dinner with your girlfriend which found its way on to your expense account, everyone does it, don't they?

We all know that offices go through ballpoint pens, envelopes, highlighters and so on at five times the rate these things actually get used in the office. And which of us can put our hand on our heart and swear we've never made a personal call on the office phone?

That's the way people in business behave. We're in business, so we behave that way too. Few of us question this.

The next few pages may make uncomfortable reading. Corporate responsibility and business ethics *do* make sound financial sense. We have looked at many reasons why, and we shall be looking at many more. But they are not things which can be imposed on a company in the same way as a new marketing strategy. If they are not done from conviction, they just won't work. You cannot act ethically unless you feel ethical. We want you to stop thinking of business as something separate, and to look at the whole of your life, of which business is just one part.

We are *not* going to advise you to cut down the time you spend working. We know how important work is, as the primary source of a man's identity, and of the identity of increasing numbers of women, and a successful business needs committed people.

Before the industrial revolution, families worked together to produce the things they needed for their survival. But once the home stopped being the workplace, things changed. Since then, business has been seen as something quite separate from the rest of life. In Dickens's *Great Expectations* the law clerk, Wemmick, became 'twin Wemmicks'. He had Walworth sentiments (Walworth was his home) and work sentiments.

The separation probably peaked in the middle years of this century, when the corporate ethos really took hold. Companies required absolute loyalty, and woe betide the man who refused a job transfer because of family commitments. But as more women entered the workforce, they became better able to appreciate the demands of business. Where before a wife may have left her husband, despairing of ever seeing him for more than a few hours a week, now she may fill the gap by taking the same route herself. It is often said that business is a more demanding mistress than any woman.

But we don't think that the solution to this divide, this gulf between life in and out of work, is to spend more time on life and less on work. We think the solution is to bring the two together.

The man or woman who looks at you in the mirror in the morning is the same man or woman carving up the opposition at the planning meeting at noon.

The man or woman carving up the opposition at the planning meeting at noon is the same man or woman who spends the lunch break visiting a sick uncle in hospital.

The man or woman who spends the lunch break visiting a sick uncle in hospital is the same man or woman who takes the tough decision to lay off fifty workers to save the jobs of five hundred more.

The man or woman who takes the tough decision to lay off fifty workers to save the jobs of five hundred more is the same man or woman who weeps on the shoulder of their partner at the loss of a favourite dog....

You are the same person, whatever you are doing. Dr Jekyll and Mr Hyde are the same man. It comes back to feeling good about yourself.

We all do things we don't feel good about – and in **The Ethics Test** (page 81) we shall ask you to list them. The way we manage to live with them is through the mechanism of *denial*.

Denial has its uses. When a loved one dies, the first reaction is denial. This allows us to cope with the immediate necessities, such as calling the doctor and making funeral arrangements. Once these tasks are done, the denial mechanism fades out and the grieving process can begin.

On a more mundane level, denial is what allows us to do things we are not really happy about without it affecting our day-to-day living. But we don't solve a problem by pretending it isn't there.

The result is stress, of both mind and body. And when you are stressed, you underperform. Not all stress is bad, of course. Most top businessmen recognize that they need that 'edge' to give of their best. The boss who is *too* relaxed risks losing out.

But the stress which is caused by denial is harmful. The damage can show in a dozen different ways: the stiff neck, the knots in your shoulders are the simplest forms. Days lost through backache cost British business millions of pounds a year, and backache is a very common manifestation of stress.

Many smokers claim the main reason they smoke is to relieve stress. What does that smoking cost the National Health Service – and the businesses whose taxes support it? And hundreds of thousands of businessmen use alcohol as a way of coping with their stress: we've already seen what that can cost.

Burn-out is becoming a commonplace term in the City. The bright ones get out before they have to. But even if they stop well short of a nervous breakdown, still they will show some symptoms of stress.

Science is only beginning to discover the extent of the power the mind has over the body. The human brain is virtually unexplored territory – and the new frontiers of medicine are going to be learning how to harness the powers of the mind to improve the health of the body. Homeopathy, aromatherapy, reflexology – all these are founded on the belief that body and mind are interconnected. You can't heal one bit in isolation.

But how is this relevant to people in business? It's straightforward. If you act the same way in business as you act at home, you should feel good about yourself. If you're feeling good about yourself, you won't be stressed. If you're not stressed, you'll work better and enjoy life more.

And as you begin to bring the different parts of your life together, something else will happen. Personal growth, one of the main things 'inner-directeds' want out of life. Personal growth starts when you begin really to care about what sort of person you are; when you want to be valued for the kind of person you are as well as the job you hold. A strong sense of self-worth is the greatest gift anyone can give their child. But if you weren't lucky enough to be given one, you can develop it.

If you spend most of your waking hours at work, you want that time to be as productive as possible. It makes sense to use that time to enrich yourself as well as your business. Doing one doesn't stop you doing the other.

Leadership

Leaders are one of the vital assets of a business. And as more of the brightest and best choose self-employment, leadership is going to become an ever more sought after quality. Apart from the technical skills, what makes a leader? She or he needs to be a good communicator – and that requires self-confidence. She needs to accept responsibility, individual as well as corporate, and to have the ability to admit 'the buck stops here'. We believe that this works two ways: the individual who accepts responsibility is likely to grow into a leader. And the third key factor in leadership is *vision*: the ability to see the big picture, and project it into the future.

Leadership is not confined to the men or women at the top, though. It is sometimes confused with rank, or with some

magical quality of charisma. But in reality leadership takes many
forms and can be found at every level within a work force. Many
employees at all levels embody the qualities of leadership, but
are not seen as leaders because of their subordinate positions.
With a change of attitude – both on the part of management and
of the employees themselves – these leaders could be encouraged to grow within their jobs, to take on more responsibility
and to take the initiative for positive change within the
company.

**Managing change is probably the biggest single concern of
top executives. And if you as an individual open yourself to
change in your personal life – and personal growth is all about
accepting and managing personal change – then you will be a
much more effective executive.**

Another way in which you will see a return from behaving
responsibly is that by helping your company identify the issues
which affect the community at large you will also be identifying
some of those which affect you. Even if they do not seem
immediately relevant, ageing, retirement, health and disable-
ment are concerns which sooner or later affect us all.

If from your position of individual responsibility you choose
to work for a responsible company, or to encourage your
present company to be more responsible, you are likely to find
that your job security is increased, and your opportunities for
promotion greater. A healthy company is a growing company,
and therefore a successful one.

As the company has responsibilities towards the stakeholders,
so too does the individual. You have personal obligations
towards the customers, shareholders and other employees which
transcend your obligations to your employers.

If you work in a food factory, and you know that one batch of
food is poisonous, you have an ethical duty to stop that batch going
out, even if management refuses to do anything. If you assemble
motor cars, and you know that the brake drums are faulty, you
have to stop that car going on the road. Going public in this kind of
situation is termed *whistle-blowing*. It can be one of the most

difficult problems you'll come across in your business career. What are the things for which *you* would put your job on the line?

'No surprises' is the motto of many successful managers. In the next section is a framework for thinking the unthinkable. Work out your strategy at a personal level for coping with whistle-blowing. Then you will be better able to work it out for your company.

Taking responsibility for your own life in this way can seem a lot tougher than taking responsibility for a major business. But remember that businesses are made up of people. The more individuals there are acting as good citizens within a business, the more good corporate citizens there will be.

Men and women with self-respect treat other people with respect. And respect is perhaps the most important single factor in human interaction. Do as you would be done by: if you respect the person sitting across the negotiating table, you will negotiate with them ethically.

Just as petty pilfering and dishonest behaviour can become a way of life, so can treating each other with respect and behaving honestly. Too many companies are either trapped in a downward spiral of behaviour, where unethical dealing is accepted as a way of life, or floundering about on the middle ground, with no clear vision of the principles by which they want to live.

The next section looks now at how to get on the upward spiral. Ethics are the key, and you may wish to move directly to the chapters on ethics. Meanwhile, we will show some of the ways in which you can put corporate responsibility into practice.

CHAPTER FIVE

WAYS TO MAKE A DIFFERENCE

Health

In the mid-1980s some American companies did their sums and came up with a frightening result. If health costs continued to escalate at the current rate, by the year 2000 *all* of their profits would be eaten up in supporting the health of their employees.

Health care is of course a major employee benefit in the United States. Workers and their families are normally insured by the company as part of their benefit package, just as National Insurance contributions are paid direct by employees and employers in the United Kingdom. But whether health care is funded by the state or by Blue Cross, it has to be paid for. And what these American companies realized was that expenditure on health care was likely to be out of control within a decade.

The threat has not disappeared entirely, but health care programmes put in place on the principle that prevention is better than cure have had a significant effect already in the United States. Increases in incidence of heart disease and cancers are slowing down, and many other benefits in decreased absenteeism and increased productivity are becoming evident.

As companies pare down their staff levels to the minimum, it becomes all the more imperative that key people should not be absent unexpectedly for long periods. This is a major part of the rationale behind private health insurance in the UK, but it is obviously better if the illness can be avoided in the first place.

Consider the following areas:

■ **Food**. Everybody has to eat, and the workplace can be an excellent place to learn new eating habits. The link between diet and health is now so well documented it does not need repeating here. Bring in a dietitian to look at menus in the company canteen. Don't change everything overnight, but make sure there is a healthy alternative. Make sure, too, that there is a good vegetarian alternative available: there are now three million people in the UK who do not eat meat, and many more who eat it infrequently.

Teach your employees about food values. Have a nutritionist demonstrate them. Being shown a glass half full of sugar and being told that it came out of just one can of cola has far greater impact than reading a leaflet. So does seeing a test tube full of salt which came out of a king-size hamburger.

Remember drink, too. The caffeine in coffee might be welcome first thing in the morning, but by afternoon some people might prefer the alternative of herb tea or decaffeinated coffee.

■ **Exercise**. Your aim should be to make this part of the company ethos, and the easiest way to do this is for top management to be seen to practice what they preach. Ideally, all new offices and factories should have exercise space, perhaps a small gym and a jogging track built in, but, failing that, most companies have some room where they could hold exercise classes before work or in the lunch hour.

Try to offer a variety of classes: jazz dance for the young and active, gentle stretching for the more sedentary. Tai Ch'i is particularly good for older workers. Yoga brings benefits in releasing tension as well as improving body function.

Measure the results. Don't hold compulsory weigh-ins, but have the company doctor check blood pressure and perhaps cholesterol levels every few months.

It is useful if you can provide showers, and hairdryers, and space to store a change of clothes. This encourages those employees who are able to do so to walk or jog to work.

■ **Stress**. Your employees' emotional health can affect their performance as much as physical health. Classes in relaxation and deep breathing are a simple place to start. Meditation may sound more esoteric, but a good teacher can show simple techniques which allow the harassed manager to clear his mind in three or four minutes and get on with decision making.

A company counsellor, attached to the personnel department, can prove extremely cost-effective. This should be a qualified and experienced person whom employees can approach in total confidence to discuss concerns which are not work-related but which are affecting their performance. It is vital that confidentiality is maintained, but without discussing individual cases the counsellor can provide very valuable feedback to the personnel director about issues which concern the workforce.

■ **Screening**. Offer well-woman check-ups to your female employees, and confidential medical check-ups for the males. It is well documented that men are more reluctant to go to doctors for what are seen as trivial complaints, and an opportunity to do this in company time could be an important way to prevent more serious illness developing.

■ **Alcohol**. Make sure you have a company policy on alcohol. An alcoholic employee can do a lot of damage, but he or she won't seek help if they think it means losing their job. Sacking helps nobody: the family at home may suffer as there may be no income, and from the company's point of view it is uneconomic, since it then has to start recruiting and training someone new. While a well-constructed alcohol policy is a humane and positive step, it is in no way a soft option. Refusal of help could mean the disciplinary procedure being invoked. In return for providing support, the company is entitled to expect a strong commitment to staying sober from the employee.

■ **Smoking**. As much of the company as possible should be smoke-free. Staff who do not smoke should not be expected to sit next to those who do. The canteen should certainly be a no-smoking zone, with immediate cost savings on cleaning. Help should be offered to employees who wish to stop, perhaps by organizing support groups or by offering consultations with a hypnotist.

Education

This is a major way in which a company can make its mark. It has two dimensions: educating the community about the company; and establishing links between the company and all levels of formal and informal educational institutions. One of the areas which the UK could well develop is interchange between business and higher education. In most other countries it is commonplace to find individuals moving between a university or college post and work in the 'real world': this obviously brings the two much closer together.

This could happen not only in business, but also in the professions and the civil service. Consistent with ethical considerations (it is not suggested that the Permanent Secretary at the Ministry of Defence take employment with a major defence contractor) great value to all parties in such interchange can be envisaged.

- **Secondment**. One of the principal benefits of seconding managers and staff to community groups is the greater understanding of business which is created. When we come to discuss some of the difficulties which arise in working with community groups we shall show that many of these difficulties arise from simple lack of knowledge about how business operates.
- **DECollege**. Digital Equipment has founded its own college with an endowment of £1,000,000 with the purpose of increasing understanding of the benefits of information technology (IT). While they also hope to meet future recruitment needs from this initiative, Geoff Shingles, DEC's Chief Executive, believes that it is in his company's interest to invest this money just to increase public awareness of what IT can do. DEC also hope to enlist other

companies working in the same field to join with them.

Even if your business cannot run to this sort of sum, you may find that through linking with your competitors you can increase the overall market by improving awareness of the benefits of your product.

■ **Schools liaison**. Schools are the source of your future employees, customers, suppliers and shareholders. It is in your interest as well as theirs to keep close to the schools. Many of these arrangements fall down, though, because it is not always possible to trade like for like.

For example, a local authority arranged for some of its teachers to gain a week's work experience in industry. This worked extremely well, and they came back to the schools with much information to pass on. But when they invited the companies to send managers to the schools to reciprocate, they found that the managers could not be spared from their jobs. This led the schools to feel that the venture was not really a success.

It always boils down to communication, of course. Information about the company's priorities was not made clear to the schools, who had assumed that if the trade could work one way it could work the other. How could this be solved?

One possibility is for the company to persuade its recently retired managers to do a stint in the schools. They have all the information about how business works, but without the time pressures of currently employed managers. Another way is for business to encourage its staff to become school governors. That way they can keep in touch with school concerns, and arrange input from the companies as appropriate.

■ **Shadowing** is a growing way of allowing young people to learn about life in business. The shadow is attached to a member of staff, and simply follows them in what they do for a period of time. They don't participate, they just observe. This can do more to educate school children about working life than a dozen lessons from a careers teacher.

■ **Endowment**. Endowing a university chair is an expensive exercise, but can be valuable. Apart from the public relations benefits, it may mean that research can be directed into an area which interests you at less cost than establishing your own facilities. The links which you will retain and develop with that professor's department will aid you in recruitment. Or simply funding a specific research project by a educational institution (rather than a commercial company) can bring these benefits to a lesser degree.

Recruitment and Retention

These are linked issues: the policies you put in place to enable you to meet your recruitment requirements are the ones which will allow you to retain good people. In the same way that American companies realized that health was the major issue for them a few years ago, recruitment should be the primary concern of British business today.

The demographics have already been spelled out: the traditional sources of employment are drying up fast, and those who fit the familiar profile are going to be able to pick and choose. How can you beat the shortage?

■ **Shared values** are the key. The theme of this book is that life and business are part of the same whole. The company which embodies the values of its employees is the company they will want to work for. But you do still have to start off with a competitive salary.
■ **Emphasize** your non-financial benefits in your recruitment advertising. Gimmicks such as holding interviews on Concorde may bring you new recruits, but unless your company can offer more than money you won't keep them.
■ **Examine your recruitment policies**. Evaluate whether each of your current requirements is absolutely necessary. If you are having difficulty finding secretaries, are you sure your advertisements are not specifying tight age limits? (70% of

secretarial ads do.) If you can't recruit part-timers, can you alter your shift patterns? You may find that starting or finishing fifteen minutes earlier to allow for school schedules is all that's needed.

Are those GCSEs you are asking for really needed? It saves the personnel department time in administering aptitude tests, but formal qualifications are not the only indication of ability. And if you look more closely at the results of the aptitude tests, you may be able to identify gaps which can be closed by specific training.

Can you encourage prospective employees to market themselves better? The woman who has been 'only a housewife' for ten years may have enormous expertise in financial management, if perhaps she has been running a voluntary organization which she has not thought to mention on her c.v. The voluntary sector in this country turns over hundreds of million pounds a year, mostly administered by people outside the formal work force.

- **Realize that returners have special needs**. Many of these needs will be discussed in the section on equal opportunities, and are common to a lot of women workers, but have you considered what you can do to attract back experienced, trained staff? The simple way to find out is to ask. Do a survey of your ex-employees, if you can find them, and also survey those of your present employees who may be thinking of taking time at home in the next few years. Needs vary by community and locality, but probably include child care, flexible working hours and shift patterns, and re-entry training.
- **Build links with local schools and colleges**. This was discussed in the previous section as an educational issue, but it is also vital for recruitment. This is how you ensure you get a work force with the skills you want.
- **Find out why your employees are leaving.** Keep statistics on how many are leaving, and why. Hold exit interviews. Use a skilled interviewer to discover the real reason for leaving, which may not be the apparent one. The woman leaving to

have a baby might have stayed if you had crèche facilities. The man going to a rival company for an extra two thousand a year might have stayed if you had offered him the training programme he was really after. Find out why they leave, and then you will know how to prevent them doing so.

- **Lastly, please don't kidnap your potential recruits.** Some Japanese firms are so desperate for good graduates that they hold interviews on the day before their competitors and literally kidnap the graduates, flying them off for a couple of days' holiday so that they miss the other interviews! We wouldn't recommend this. Not ethical.

Training

A recent report from Hay Management Consultants suggests that one of the most effective ways for employers to attract full-timers to work for them will be by offering training as a recruitment incentive. As we said before, it has to be seen in its proper place, not as a sticking plaster to patch over the worries of an unhappy employee, but as a factor of critical importance in recruitment, retention and job satisfaction.

Highly qualified staff have the potential to be highly mobile: they are aware of their needs for constant stimulation and development. Training programmes must address these needs:

- **Get the right courses for the right people.** This is not as obvious as it sounds. Any trainer will tell you how often they hear members of a course complaining that they have no idea why they are sitting there. Training is full of good intentions gone wrong.
- **Involve the employee.** Of course the training courses have to be relevant to the company's needs, but you also have to consider the individual's aspirations and needs. Once you have identified each side's needs, then you can match them.
- **Use the performance appraisal to do this.** You do have one of these at least once a year, don't you? Performance

appraisals are a two-way communication – or should be. Manager and employee sit down and work out where the employee is now and where he wants to be by the time of the next appraisal. The difference between point A and point B identifies the training need.

- **Gather all the expressed training needs together.** In the course of the interview, a good manager will have guided the employee away from areas which have no relevance to the needs of the company. (But he will have made a mental note to tell the human resources people that these are areas of concern to employees, and should therefore be examined.)
- **Then take the skills needs identified by senior management, and link the two together.** By approaching training from this angle you will reach a solution which supports the individual at the same time as it supports the company.
- **Use secondment as a training resource.** Once upon a time a computer company seconded a sales manager to a London borough for a year: he had had a skiing accident, and had to wear a neck support which made a mobile job difficult. The borough put him to work teaching local small businesses about information technology. He therefore learned a great deal about the needs of small business in the IT field. Just as his year was up, his company announced its move into the personal computer market: this sales manager was then perfectly placed to give vital information about customer requirements to the company.

  We can't always be quite so lucky in the interchange, but just as communities can learn from business, so can business people learn valuable lessons from their time in the community.

- **Develop re-entry training programmes.** These both support the community in enabling older women to return to work and help meet the company's recruitment needs.
- **Make your training programmes available to members of the community at large.** Very often a company will run an internal training or management development programme with less than maximum numbers. One or two people drop

out at the last minute; the course runs anyway. Where a company has a good long-term relationship with a community group, it may be appropriate to offer the training place to a member of that group who is available at short notice.

■ **Don't forget assertiveness training.** This has value for employees both at work, in enhancing negotiation skills and improving relationships within the office, and in their home life, enabling them to put the same tools to use. It is not just for women – men often need to be taught that aggression is not assertiveness.

The environment

Care for the environment is what first springs to mind in any discussion about corporate responsibility. We see companies taking natural resources and using them for profit, and we feel that they have a duty to care for these resources and dispose safely of waste products. The return for the company which cares for the environment is greatly increased customer loyalty. It is a very public issue, and failure to meet the community's expectations leads to greater media publicity than any other part of business's social obligations. It is also an area highly prone to government intervention if companies are not seen to be self-regulating.

These suggestions are not aimed at dealing with the major large scale problems – the kind which are usually dealt with by legislation, such as that which is causing Ciba Geigy to spend £296 million over the next four years on reducing pollution from its manufacturing units in Switzerland. They are directed at areas which affect us all – every business person: areas where we can make a big impact with fairly small changes to the way we do things.

■ **Start with the company itself.** The external design of the buildings – the architecture. Does this reflect both the company's purpose and the visual expectations of the local community?

- **When commissioning new buildings or plant,** make sure that the architect's brief includes consultation with community groups. It should also specify incorporation wherever possible of ecologically sound alternatives.

- **More likely, you're stuck with the premises you have.** See what cosmetic alterations you can make to give the exterior a more attractive appearance – a relatively small amount spent on landscaping, window boxes or plants on balconies can bring big improvements in the public perception of your company.

- **Then look at the inside of your premises.** It is not for nothing that the Japanese are so fanatical about tidiness. They know it brings increases in productivity. Do your staff look around them and see cheerful, pleasant surroundings which bring a smile to their faces?

- **Tidiness applies outside, too.** If you are in the fast food business, we assume you have lots of litter bins outside the premises. But that is not enough – make sure a member of staff goes out regularly with a long handled dustpan to pick up the rubbish that misses the bins. It's no use blaming the public. Unless they see you caring, they won't care either.

- **Packaging is the major polluter.** Is it all really necessary? Could you staple or sellotape receipts to goods which are already packaged rather than putting them in bags?

- **Build in environmental considerations as a fundamental part of the product design process.** Make sure that your company examines all the alternatives. This applies to services too. Always examine the Green alternative.

- **Convert your company cars to take lead free petrol.** You'll also save money on this. If they can't be converted, buy different models next time round.

- **Look at using recycled paper,** at least for internal memos. We know that it's not so attractive or businesslike, but there may be places you can use it.

- **Make sure your canteen sends its bottles to the Bottle Bank.** Aluminium cans can also be recycled without too much trouble.
- **Tell your cleaning contractors that you want them to use bio-degradeable materials and CFC-free aerosols.** There are plenty of alternatives on the market.
- **Remember noise pollution.** Keep noise levels down. This also lessens a major source of stress for your work force.
- **Examine your purchasing policies.** Can you specify a Green alternative? If two suppliers are offering the same deal, do you give preference to the one who cares more for the environment?

Equal opportunities

There is Equal Opportunities legislation on the statute book. But a real equal opportunities policy recognizes that some people start with a handicap. In this section, we intend to show ways to remove some of those handicaps.

Equal opportunities do not concern only women. Advertisements proclaim so-and-so to be an equal opportunities employer, who welcomes applications from ethnic minorities and disabled people as well as women. Interestingly, that same employer may be denying someone else the equal opportunity simply because of their age. Ageism will be the next frontier in equal opportunity legislation, and we shall be discussing that under the heading of retirement.

But many of the concerns relate to women, with whom we shall start:

- **Appoint an Equal Opportunities executive.** Ideally, this person should be at a senior level so that she or he can make a real contribution to strategy. Their remit should be to examine all issues which prevent potential staff from joining the company, existing staff from staying in it and upward movement of staff through the company.

The reporting line of your EO executive depends on whether you see equal opportunities as a marketing device or a recruitment tool. Most companies see it as an issue which affects recruitment, retention and employee relations, and therefore place it within the human resources function.

■ **Find out what your employees' real child care needs are.** Too often it is assumed that crèche facilities are all that is needed, when very often care of 5-12 year olds is a far greater problem. At least care demands of the under-fives are predictable. It is much easier to find full-time care on a regular basis than part-time care for forty weeks a year and full-time for the holidays.

Holiday play schemes are easy to organize. Parents' productivity will rise dramatically when they stop worrying about young children left at home unsupervised. Employees' home telephone bills will drop, too. Hundreds of thousands of young children are left at home alone after school and in holiday time: not all of them are sitting quietly reading or watching TV. Helping your work force in this way is also helping society.

■ **Give part-timers the same working conditions as full-timers.** If you want a loyal, committed work force you have to treat them all the same. Most women working part-time are doing it for the convenience of other people, not themselves. They are doing it because they can't find good child care. They are doing it because their husbands still expect the housework to be done for them. They are doing it because they need the money. They are doing it because they're fed up with apologising for being 'just a housewife'.

Giving people more responsibility encourages them to behave more responsibly. A woman working part-time earns on average £2.96 an hour. If she were working full time, she would earn £3.84. (Her male equivalent, incidentally, would be earning £5.21: 1988 figures from the Equal Opportunities Commission.)

It's an easy argument that if the employer values you less,

you give him less. Don't let your staff take that attitude towards you.

- **Open more jobs to job-share.** One of the hardest things for many part-timers to accept is that because they cannot work the conventional 35 or 40 hour week they are expected to work well below their capabilities and qualifications.

   A headteacher who wants to work part-time will usually end up as a supply teacher. A senior nursing sister may get no more than the well-paid tedium of agency nursing; and a full-time department manager will be lucky to find anything more than secretarial work on a part-time basis.

Job share *works*. Provided it is well thought through and enough cross-over time is allowed, the company can benefit from the most productive working time of both partners. Two halves add up to more than one whole. And cover is automatically there for sickness and holidays. Even senior jobs can work on this basis, with enough careful planning.

- **Allow flexible working wherever possible.** In the last three years one quarter of UK employers have introduced 'flex-itime'. As well as helping employees to balance their home and work commitments, it increases productivity.

- **Be alert for sexual harassment.** The latest US survey estimates that sexual harassment costs the average Fortune 500 company $7 million a year. These are costs in absentee-ism and increased turnover, not direct law suits. Two-thirds of the same group of companies had had formal complaints laid against them.

   Discuss this issue in your code of ethics and have clear procedures laid down for employees to follow. Take firm action to deal with reported incidents – they are probably only the tip of the iceberg. Remember that men can suffer too. This is an area where whistle-blowing is to be encouraged. Make *everyone* aware of the rules.

   This also needs to be dealt with by education. It is not necessarily harassment for a senior female manager to be called 'dear' by a man (who is just as likely to be the caretaker as her boss), but it is both demeaning and unprofessional.

That it comes across in this way just would not occur to many men.

It is also important for male staff to be made aware of the language they use on the telephone, and of their assumptions when they hear a female voice at the other end. Not all women are secretaries or take kindly to being called 'love' by a stranger. They may be major customers who could take their business elsewhere. Remember, 43% of business start-ups in the UK are by women.

- **Introduce a mentor programme.** Mentoring is a traditional way for young men to learn about the intangibles which will earn them promotion – the corporate ethos. Women and ethnic minority groups are usually excluded from the informal network within which this operates. Formally assigning an older, more experienced staff member to act as a mentor can give the young black or woman (or, most disadvantaged of all, young black woman!) a chance to learn about these important matters.

  Making it formal, too, takes away one of the concerns of senior male executives who might otherwise extend a hand of friendship to young women. They are less likely to generate rumours of sexual impropriety if the assignment is made by the personnel department.

- **Acknowledge that your employees have other respon-sibilities in their lives.** Do not force women to call in sick because one of their children is sick, or an elderly parent needs care. Surveys at American Express and AT&T discovered that between 30% and 60% of employees were concerned about the conflict between work and domestic responsibilities. The majority believed their work perfor-mance would be improved if their employers introduced family-oriented services and policies.

  These could include free resource and referral services about local child care facilities, financial contributions towards the cost of caring for children and elderly parents; on-site crèches and after-school programmes for 'latch-key' children; and provision of care for mildly sick children, either through home nursing, a day-care centre or a hospital bed. Penguin Books, for example, allows parents of either sex 15 days paid leave to look after sick children.

- **Educate your personnel people in cultural differences which may lead them unwittingly to discriminate against members of ethnic minorities.** An interviewee from some cultures, for example, may stand or sit at a distance which the interviewer finds uncomfortably close: the interviewee, on the other hand, may feel that to sit further away could cause offence.
- **Aptitude tests set to potential new recruits should be screened for cultural bias.** It is very easy for these to be based on assumptions which are not common to everyone.
- **Make sure your premises are accessible to people with disabilities.** The legal liability on larger employers to employ a quota of 3% of disabled people is honoured more in the breach than the observance. But while you are waiting for your toilets to be adapted.
- **Examine ways in which telecommuting could be used to provide work at home for those who have difficulty getting out.** There is no doubt that telecommuting will be a major growth area. Most of the reservations expressed about it relate to the lack of social contact. Try looking at it, however, as a means of widening the horizons of people with disabilities, who might otherwise have little contact with the outside world.

Retirement and older workers

Ideas about age and retirement are changing. The Secretary of State for Employment has forecast that before too long the retirement age may be raised to 70. Because in the past companies have needed to make room for new young employees they have assumed that older employees should leave at a certain age. Now that there are no longer so many young people pushing at the doors, the whole principle of retirement should be questioned. Longer life expectancy and better health into old age are also relevant factors.

- **Do not make judgments about anybody solely on the basis of their age.** Always look at their ability to do the job. There is likely to be legislation about this within the next decade, in any case, and if your policies are already clear you won't have a problem. Age is often used as a shorthand in recruitment advertising for a certain level of experience or a salary indicator – if that is what you mean, why not say so?

    There are very few jobs where age is a vital criterion. It may have been useful in the past to specify age as a sifting tool, but as the pool of people with the skills and experience you need gets smaller you need to throw the net wider.

- **Allow your employees to choose, within reason, when they want to retire.** Performance is what matters, and provided they can still perform to agreed limits you should allow them to do so.

- **Look at ways of introducing phased retirement.** Job sharing can be just as valid for the over-60s as for young mothers. Negotiate with your older employees to establish how many hours' work a week suits them and you.

- **Don't neglect training for your older workers.** You are prepared to invest heavily in training for young graduates, many of whom may leave you within a few years. Older workers are less mobile and have greater loyalty to the company – the investment will surely repay itself.

- **Make sure retirement is not seen as a threat.** The best way to do this is to give your employees something to look forward to, such as the community volunteer programme discussed earlier.

- **Honour the experience of your older employees.** Long service awards can be highly prized, if given with sensitivity and respect.

- **And make use of that experience.** Employees who have been with the company for a long time are the guardians of the company's ethos. Use them as an informal sounding board for new plans and programmes.

Arts and sports sponsorship

This is often seen as one of the most important commitments of business to the community. There can be little doubt that many arts and sports organizations owe their success – indeed their very survival – to business sponsorship. We have to applaud the resources that companies allocate to this purpose.

There may, however, be mixed feelings about this, owing to the fact that many people in the community are confused about the objectives of such sponsorship, and sometimes the confusion is evident even within the donor companies.

We would argue for a clearer distinction between sponsorship of arts and sports activities as support for the community, and the kind of marketing-driven sponsorship which has the primary purpose of promoting a company through channels to which its products would not normally be given access. We do not dispute that there is a strong case to be made for this kind of support on marketing grounds alone. However, operations of this nature would not fall under the heading of corporate responsibility, and therefore are not an appropriate subject for discussion on these pages. We believe that it will be from time to time very much in a company's interests to support arts and sports activities in order to demonstrate its commitment to the community.

This would be done primarily with the objective of community support and not as a measure to avoid media prohibition on advertising certain products to certain audiences. This may seem an academic point: nevertheless, in any serious discussion on corporate responsibility we feel it is a distinction which has to be drawn.

For companies wishing to sponsor arts organizations in line with their corporate objectives, the best starting point may be the Association for Business Sponsorship of the Arts: sports sponsorship is generally handled through the governing bodies of the various sports. The whole question of amateur status in sport is currently under debate. Companies which wish to sponsor individuals are likely to find in future that devices such as setting up trusts will be unnecessary: this should encourage more sponsorship of this kind.

Charitable giving (corporate philanthropy)

This is another area which is growing fast in the United Kingdom. One of the best and most tax efficient ways of giving is to enlist the help of the Charities Aid Foundation, who have considerable expertise in matching charitable giving with corporate objectives.

CHAPTER SIX

PUTTING IT INTO PRACTICE

THE STARTING POINT is finding out where you are now. We believe that most companies already contribute to the community in some way. The difficulty lies in identifying that expenditure. Very often it is split among a large number of budgets. Some is in public relations; some in personnel; some in the Chairman's contingency fund; some with the Finance Director: if you look across the company, you may identify as many as twenty or thirty different sources of corporate responsibility expenditure.

Each branch, division or factory within your company is being approached all the time. *The chances are that you are responding to these approaches, but in an undirected, unstrategic way.*

The second task of the initial survey is to find out where your staff think priorities lie. Ask for the views of your people about the issues important to their community. Simply asking these questions gets your managers thinking in the long term about community issues, so that when you start developing your strategy they will be better placed to contribute to it.

Past patterns will have to be built in to the new strategy: it is vital that the process should be seen as adding to the company's role as a good citizen, rather than subtracting from it. The last thing you should do is make a head office decision to withdraw support from a local organization a branch office has been funding for years.

Be wary if you choose to conduct this survey yourself, rather than bringing in a specialist consultant. It is possible to set a member of staff the task of identifying the expenditure, but it is not easy for an insider to come up with the right answers. Particularly in a medium-to-large company, many senior people have a small 'slush' fund which they like to keep quiet, and they would not be keen on revealing this to the Chairman's PA.

And while the answers to some of the questions will be financial, it is not a task to set an accountant. This is a difficult area to quantify and measure, and needs considerable background in the field to identify the relevant issues. It is not expensive to call in experts. For a medium-sized company, say 500 employees, an initial review, presented together with thoughts on future strategy, should not take more than a month and would cost considerably less than, say, reviewing pay scales.

When you know where you are now, you can start planning where you are going.

Purpose

The first question to ask is, *'What is the purpose of this organization?'* This may seem a silly question at first sight. If your business is a new one and you are the founder, you know what your purpose is. But often as companies grow and develop the original answer becomes less clear.

This is a guide to developing a structure which will enable you to identify the ways in which you can run a responsible, profitable business which people will want to work for. But until you have defined your purpose we cannot help you to work out the objectives, strategies and processes which form that structure. These must be born out of the purpose of the organization.

In the section on business ethics we discuss the crucial importance of the purpose. It needs to be stated and communicated, and the commitment of both managers and employees to that purpose must be gained.

Defining the purpose is a task for the Managing Director. He may well consult with his board on this; at the end, he should come up with a simple statement, such as: "Our purpose is to provide good products and services, profitably, to a wide customer base." Each company's purpose is different: it will probably include the specific product or service area, but it should be stated as simply as possible.

The objectives, strategies and processes will help in turn to define what is right for the business, that is, to establish the appropriate areas of corporate responsibility. *No one company can be expected to meet all of the needs of the community, nor even most of them. The object of this model is to enable you to define those specific needs which can be met to your mutual benefit.* Many of the examples we have given above were responses based on a very clear understanding of the purpose of the organization and of its needs.

Following this process will indicate to you what your company needs from the community, and will help to determine the interconnections between those needs and what the company is currently providing.

Identify the stakeholders

Everybody who is affected by your business is a stakeholder: shareholders, obviously; employees, including former employees to whom you pay pensions; customers; suppliers; the community at large – both your local community and the wider national or global community whom your actions can affect. You may have other specific groups whose interests you need to consider.

State the company's objectives

The Managing Director's job here is to state them responsibly, taking the interests of all these groups into account as fairly as possible.

What is the objective for the **shareholders?** The answer is probably to provide a reasonable return on their investment.

For the **staff?** To manage and reward them fairly; to communicate well with them; to involve them in the company's operations.

For the **customers?** To care for them, and to serve their interests as far as possible.

For the **suppliers?** To be fair and honourable in all dealings with them.

For the **community at large?** To seek to operate in line with the community's best interests and act as a good corporate citizen.

All these are only examples. Each company needs to examine itself and its purpose so that it can set its own objectives.

Out of these examples, the company can develop strategies.

Define the strategies

As before, we give examples of how these may emerge.

For the **shareholders:** to manage the company effectively to provide an agreed rate of return on their investment, and to set goals for each department in order to achieve this.

For the **staff:** the personnel department will address their needs in line with the company's objectives.

For the **customers:** to provide quality products and services at competitive prices; to write a customer charter; to seek to market the products and services as effectively as possible.

For the **suppliers:** likewise, to contract with them to provide quality services to the company and properly to compensate them for so doing.

For the **community at large:** to ensure the company is sensitive to the impact of its products on the environment; to engage in activities which support and strengthen the community; to seek to avoid activities which militate against the community's interests.

Once the strategies are defined, it is possible to identify the processes which will enable the objectives to be achieved.

Identify the processes

We choose next to examine the processes rather than the goals, which would be the conventional follow-on from the strategy. Goals are static and need to be re-stated regularly.

The best models of organizational development are flow models, which recognize that change is constant and intrinsic. Managing change is about managing a process, not a series of static points. The static points are markers along the way: their purpose is to measure where one is at a given point in time. Goals are needed, but processes are of the essence.

For the **shareholders:** to communicate as openly as possible with them, through the annual report and the annual general meeting, about the progress of the company.

For the **staff:** to recruit, retain and motivate staff at all levels in line with the objectives and strategies; to establish participatory career and management development programmes: to provide the best training programmes available towards that end.

For the **customers:** service and care will become a priority.

For the **suppliers:** not to buy more than an agreed percentage of their output so that they will not find themselves in difficulty should the company's requirement cease; to pay promptly; to establish a procurement policy aimed at treating suppliers fairly.

For the **community at large:** all staff and the company as a whole will behave responsibly and deal ethically with community organizations; the company will encourage community involvement by staff; it will make financial and other commitments to the community; it will encourage awareness of its products in the community, and demonstrate their advantages; it will seek to supply its products or services free or cheaply to community groups with whom it has a relationship.

The most difficult part of all this for most companies is the involvement with the community – not because it is particularly hard, but because it is unfamiliar. We therefore give below a clear model of how to go about it.

How does an organization manage its interfaces with the community?

The Concentric Circle Model

The outer circle represents the community, with points marking current issues.

The inner circle represents the company, with points marking its principal concerns.

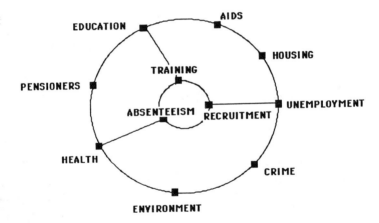

How it works:

- Do an external scan to identify the issues of concern to the community
- Now do an internal scan to identify the issues bearing upon your company
- Make the connections

No one company can do it all. Even though all the issues may affect the company in one way or another, they will not all have a measurable impact on the business. All organizations have limited resources. It is the process of prioritizing which enables the choice of how best to use those resources to be made.

In the example opposite, the company has identified its pressing concerns as recruitment, absenteeism and training. The recruitment problem is paralleled by concern within the community about levels of unemployment. In other words, there is a resource within the community – unemployed people – which could meet the needs of the company – new employees. It is a resource which cannot immediately be accessed or the two complementary needs would already have been matched up. The question then becomes a straightforward one of examining ways in which the company can help unemployed people to acquire the skills which the company requires.

The second problem identified is that of high absenteeism levels due to sickness. The complementary issue within the community is concern about health. By running positive health programmes for employees and their families, and contributing to community health in any or all of the ways outlined in our examples, the company will serve both its own needs and the community's.

The third issue on which the company chooses to focus is training – to ensure a more highly educated and capable workforce. The community is concerned that all its members should reach their maximum educational potential: links between the two can be made so that both aims are met.

This company has eliminated intervention in areas where it can see no immediate benefit to the company and does not feel able to make a response. These are areas where there is no mutual interest. There can be no social contract without a mutuality of interest.

Once the company's priorities have been identified, the next step is to establish how it intends to respond to the community needs which match these priorities:

The Inverted Triangle Model

The company starts at the bottom of the triangle and moves upwards.

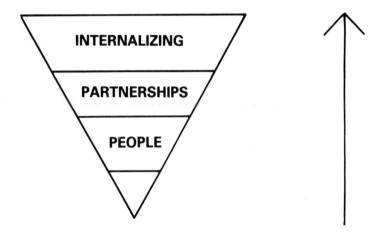

The first level is **money.** Applying money to the problem is the easiest way to respond to a community need: it may also be the least effective.

The next level is **people.** Get your people involved with the community. And start at the top. The Managing Director may be the busiest man in the company, but if he makes time to join the committee of the local youth club all the rest of the employees will get the signal that this is a good thing to do.

Even if it is not appropriate to allow individuals a few hours a week of company time to participate in voluntary organizations there are many ways in which it can be made easier and more rewarding: a central register of opportunities could be kept by the personnel department, special recognition could be made in the company paper.

This is where secondment fits in. Giving the services of a skilled manager, an accountant, a plumber or an electrician to a community group can be worth much more than money.

Your employee will both teach and learn from the community. In England and Wales the Action Resource Centre can help.

The third level is **partnerships.** Where the issues being faced are too great for any one company to make an impact, the way forward is for companies to join together to bring greater resources to bear on the problem.

The final level is both the most rewarding and the most difficult to achieve. **Internalizing** means that the lessons learned in the community are fed back into the company. This way the company retains its links with the community and enhances them, because they are constantly being reviewed. It gets everybody involved in the act.

All of your employees who are involved in the community are on a continuous training programme, as they take the lessons learned outside and feed them back in. Remember that that same community is very often your customer base. *Your public relations improve. All of your employees become ambassadors, raising not just the profile but more importantly the public perception of the company.*

Internalization shows that the company, as part of its purpose, is endorsing the values of the community through its involvement with, and commitment to, those values. It is another upward spiral. Doing good makes everyone feel good. Feeling good makes them want to do more good. Stress levels drop, commitment increases.

We cannot emphasize enough the importance of the commitment of top management to the shared purpose. Just as they are committed to achieving the financial goals of the company, they need to be seen to be committed to the corporate responsibility goals. Progress can be measured in this area as in any other. Corporate responsibility goals should be *smart* goals: Specific, Measurable, Agreed, Realistic, Timely.

How do you measure them? By the effect on the problems they set out to address, for example:

- absenteeism levels
- recruitment difficulties
- inadequately trained employees

Other important measurable results include:

- the perception of the company within the community
- the ease with which the company conducts relationships with politicians and community leaders
- the ease with which plans for change and development in the business are accepted
- the ease with which the company is able to make rapid alterations to cope with sudden changes in the market place

These effects can be plotted over time: make sure you have a base line measurement before you start to implement your new strategy.

You may find that in money terms, a corporate responsibility programme is no more expensive than a public relations or advertising programme. And while a PR programme can be guaranteed to increase the profile of your company, it cannot be guaranteed to improve its public perception. In the long run, public perception of your company will match the reality. A corporate responsibility programme, unlike PR, speaks as much to the long term as to the short.

We suggest that 1% of your gross profit is a good figure to start off with. When you do the sums, you may already be spending not far off this anyway. But the difference is that now you have prioritized your needs, and are spending in accordance with your objectives. The Chairman's secretary may have the best intentions in the world, but she is an inefficient channel through which to pass such an important part of your budget.

CHAPTER SEVEN

HOW DOES THE COMMUNITY REACT?

Recognizing differences

Business people *think* differently from members of community groups. Of course some community groups have members who are businessmen, but in the main they tend to be run by people who have little experience of commercial life.

It is vital for a business which wants to contribute to its local community to be aware of these differences and the communication problems which they can cause. We hope that this chapter will give both businesses and those who hope to benefit from developing links with them a greater understanding of how the other operates.

Different time scales can be one of the major blocks. A company which is accustomed to making a decision today and implementing it tomorrow cannot understand why a community group, asked for information which will enable the company to make a substantial donation, takes so long to respond.

Always bear in mind that community groups are almost invariably run by volunteers in their spare time. The fact that it is spare time means that many other things in their life take priority. They may meet as infrequently as once a month – if the treasurer, say, misses one meeting, then it may be two months before they are in a position to reply.

Their scheduling of meetings, too, may pose problems for business. If a company wants to send a representative to a meeting it is likely to find that this takes place out of business hours. Most groups find evenings and weekends a more convenient time.

Community groups may direct funding requests to the wrong person within a company, or even to the wrong company. These requests may be overly modest, or possibly they may grossly overestimate the capacity of the company to respond.

This is a simple consequence of lack of information about how companies operate. The best way for a business to deal with these approaches is to suggest that a member of the group comes along for a short meeting (do not hesitate to stipulate that it be short) with the appropriate employee of the company. The staff member can then outline the best way of approaching the company and perhaps offer a briefing sheet for guidance. Make it clear that this is not a situation for decision making, but rather an aid to the group so that it stands a better chance of receiving a positive response.

The form of the request, even if directed to the right person, may appear hopelessly unbusinesslike and be lacking in fundamental information. Because community groups so often depend on volunteers, they often simply do not have a full range of business skills among their members. Understandings which business people take for granted among those whom they meet on a day-to-day basis may just not be there.

A project which is enthusiastically proposed by a community group and supported by a company may lose momentum and fizzle to a stop within a few months. This can cause enormous difficulty for a company. Convinced by the community group of the importance of the project, they may have assigned substantial funding and a staff member to help it along. When a company makes a commitment of this nature, it naturally wishes to see it through until the goals are achieved.

The Chairman expects regular reports from the staff member assigned to the project. But contact with the organization becomes spasmodic and increasingly difficult. This may be caused by the departure of one particular member from the community group; or it may be that, faced with the reality of the work involved in carrying out the project, enthusiasm has simply dwindled. Motivating volunteers is a different ball-game.

Members of community groups will not think like business people and will not necessarily act like business people. Business should be as professional in its relationship with community groups as in its relationship with any other business. Be clear about your objectives and their objectives. Aim to build a long-term relationship with the groups you support. Accept that their purpose is unlikely to be the same as that of a commercial organization.

But once you have decided to back a community organization, back it to the hilt. Have faith in your own judgment. With an open-minded approach, the very differences between the commercial and the community outlook can prove very valuable to the company. There is joy in diversity. It can prevent a company becoming ossified.

There has to be value to both parties in this relationship. You are building your own version of the social contract, and everyone will benefit.

Sharing skills and building bridges

Skill sharing is a two-way process. Recognize that members of the community have skills which your company could find valuable.

People who run community groups are used to managing people over whom they have little direct control. This is a valuable and rare management skill, and will become more necessary as more organisations follow the model of the 'hollowed-out' corporation which is discussed in Chapter 9. Community leaders also need to be good motivators, and usually have the ability to elicit funds from a multiplicity of sources. They are adept at leverage.

And apart from skills, they possess information. One of the fundamentals which separates you from your competitors is the quality of your information. The community is awash with information, if you have the will to listen. Market research rarely looks at this level, which is often the key to enriching that information flow. If your customer base is your local community, your partnership will pay rich dividends.

Reverse secondment is something you should consider. One way of doing this was suggested in the training section, where we proposed making available unfilled places on company courses. The opportunity to participate in a management development course would be particularly welcomed by managers employed by voluntary organizations, who may not have the funding to pay for this.

There may be actual short-term projects within your company which could be carried out by members of community groups. In any event, if you have accommodation available, it is useful to place a room at the disposal of your community partners for their administration or meetings. It need not be a permanent room – lack of flexibility is rarely a problem with community activists.

The importance of all this is that the greater the contact between your staff and members of the community, the greater the understanding which will develop. The greater the understanding, the greater the likelihood that forms of cooperation will emerge which meet both your objectives and the community's objectives.

Bridges are built by people, not by money. The more personal contact there is between members of your company and members of the community, the stronger the bridges will be.

Be sensitive to personal differences between yourselves and others. Business people *do* dress differently, and talk differently. Don't expect carefully articulated and reasoned requests – the skills may not be there. Most of all, try not to have expectations. Try to accept what you see, and work from that starting point.

Remember there is probably also a political divide. Some groups do see life in party political terms, and are highly suspicious of business people. Perhaps they do not know many business people, and their impressions of them are formed by the media.

Encourage as many of your staff as possible to participate actively in community organizations. In many of the most successful companies it is unusual if every main board director is not involved in a community project – because successful companies recognize that we are all part of the same community.

PART II

Business Ethics

CHAPTER EIGHT

INTRODUCTION TO BUSINESS ETHICS

WE HAVE OUTLINED the 'how to' of corporate responsibility. That is very important, and if you want to you can skip the next few chapters and move on to 'Communicating the New Strategy' (page 107), a guide to communications within an organization which will complete the 'how to' part of this book. Then you will be fully equipped to incorporate socially responsible practice into your business strategy. Now, however, we want to go further.

Actions speak louder than words, and of course it matters that you practise corporate responsibility, that you *implement* programmes which meet your company's objectives in this field. In fact, later we shall argue that actions are the only thing that count when we look at how a company commits itself to an ethical way of behaving. But unless the actions are underpinned by belief, by commitment to continue to act in these ways, they will go the way of all management fashions.

Unless there is a clear commitment to corporate responsibility so that it becomes part of the company way of doing business (we don't say culture, for reasons that will become clear later), when the individuals who pushed for it move on, it will suddenly become the dispensable part of the budget. Of course this is a short-sighted view, but when pressure is on the budget, items which produce long-term as opposed to short-term returns may be the first to go.

Many companies would argue that corporate responsibility is fine for those businesses which are already successful. Once you have success then you can add on the fancy bits, the extras, like corporate responsibility. But until you've made it, or when you feel under threat, then you should concentrate on the things which *really* affect the bottom line.

We disagree. We believe that business success, and for that matter business survival, depends on the company being close not just to its customers, but to the community at large. Businesses are doomed to find themselves in difficulty when they try to distance themselves from the environment in which they operate. Society permits the effective conduct of business because it recognizes the contribution which business makes. If that recognition were ever to be withdrawn, business would have real difficulty in surviving. On the other hand, the greater that recognition and the clearer the identification between the interests of the community and of business, then the greater the chances of business success and growth.

We believe that corporate responsibility should lie at the very heart of a company's business strategies. The reason for this belief becomes clear when we examine something which is central not only to corporate responsibility, but to all of a business's operations – business ethics.

We've heard all the jokes about business ethics. We know that many people see it like military intelligence – a contradiction in terms. But the fact that the very expression 'business ethics' causes such merriment points up a very important fact. It shows how far businesses have retreated from the fundamental debate about what is happening in society today – and what will be happening tomorrow.

In the course of the next few chapters we will argue that business ethics are the key to business survival and business success. We will explain why this is so, and what businesses can do to gain what we call the **ethics edge**.

In the course of this discussion we shall also look to the future. We shall attempt to address not only how ethics can support a company in its present operations, but also how they can be used to develop the successful company of the future. We shall also be debating the paradox that corporate responsibility *is* individual responsibility, and individual responsibility *is* corporate responsibility, and we shall show that understanding and working with this paradox is the key to obtaining the commitment of entire organizations in responding to community needs.

CHAPTER NINE

ETHICS ARE THE KEY

Why should a company be ethical?

One of the best-kept legal secrets today is that a company is not owned by its shareholders. Most shareholders we know believe that they are part owners of the companies in which they hold shares. But in law the company is a distinct entity.

In 1897 the *Salomon v Salomon & Co* judgment established the principle that a corporation is something different from its members. This was reinforced in 1947 when, summing up in *Short v Treasury Commissioners*, Lord Justice Evershed said, 'shareholders are not in the eye of the law part-owners of the undertaking. The undertaking is something different from the totality of its shareholdings.' The principle that a company is a separate entity and not ownable by its shareholders also applies in Canadian and US law, as well as in Sweden and West Germany.

So if shareholders do not own a company, what is their relationship to it? The answer, we believe, lies in the original meaning of the word 'own'. In middle English, from the fourteenth to the seventeenth centuries, the word used for possession was not 'own', but 'owe'. What we would today call an 'owner' was an 'ower'.

Just as the shareholders 'owe' the company, so does the company 'owe' its component parts. The obligations of a company, what it 'owes' as distinct from what it 'owns', include its duties to *all* its stakeholders.

Up to this point we have given sound economic justification for behaving in a reponsible manner. There is also good economic justification for being ethical – especially on the large scale, where the ethical approach is the only one which gives you the tools to predict and avoid corporate tragedy on the scale of Bhopal or Guinness.

But being ethical is much more than just behaving in a responsible fashion. Being ethical is about taking individual responsibility. It is about internalizing values. In the previous section we provided a recipe for behaving responsibly. At the lower levels of our inverted triangle model, responsibility can be imposed on a company by one or two highly motivated people at the top. But until the principles are internalized, the results will be limited.

Organizations such as Business in the Community are making major advances in raising business awareness of these issues. Our task here is to offer a conceptual framework which will underpin the work already done, and enable business to move forward faster from this base.

In its crudest terms, what happens typically at present is that a business gets together with the local authority and the community to look at a particular problem. The three parties nominate a few people each to sit round a table: these people then agree a set of ground rules for their approach and go back trying to sell them. But because the bulk of people in the business are not truly involved – they see themselves as having no responsibility – they do not share in the sense of corporate responsibility expressed by the business. It is doubtful whether the community leader and the local authority representative feel fundamentally responsible for all the other players in that situation. Workers in the local authority, for example, are unlikely to feel personally responsible.

The process is being driven from the outside: it is the organizations who are forming the so-called 'partnership'. But this is a negation of true partnership. As we have stated before, *bridges are built by people,* not by money.

Without individual responsibility it is impossible to achieve full corporate responsibility. In Japan a group of individuals assembles a car door. The door is defective – the defect is in the window flashing. Worker Miko's job is to assemble the locks. The window flashing is put on by worker Hako. But when the door is shown to be faulty, worker Miko will readily say, 'I made a bad door'.

We, as members of an organization, have a collective responsibility for what we do, but this can only be exercised if as individuals we take on that responsibility. Consider these equations:

corporate responsibility = individual responsibility
individual responsibility = corporate responsibility

Who is responsible, the individual or the group? This question is at the heart of ethics. The equations above represent a paradox which we need to accept if we wish to be ethical.

We are not offering recipes in this section. We are offering an ideal, for business and for business organizations. This is where we stop being a conventional 'how to' book. We are going to supply not solutions but tools to ask the questions which will let everyone find their own way to the solutions.

It would be impertinent of us to claim to offer a blueprint which could apply equally to the individual circumstances of every business person who reads this book. You know your own business infinitely better than anybody else. But we can help you to ask the right questions in order to find the right answer for you.

Not everybody – or every company – is ready to face up to the demands made in this section. If you find that the prospect of internalizing ethical behaviour is one which you do not feel ready to cope with yet, so be it. Ethics cannot be imposed from outside.

We believe that most people want to be good most of the time. But being human means that we are fallible – and some people are out to buck the system. All the ethical behaviour in the world on the part of others won't stop an Ivan Boesky choosing to behave unethically.

Knowledge is power. We will give you the knowledge and the tools which will enable you to make the ethical choice. **But that choice lies in your own hands.**

The concepts and values we shall be discussing are more difficult to follow through than the ones we have dealt with up to now, but we shall try to explain them as simply and clearly as possible. Even if at the end you decide that it's not right for you now, we'd like you to hear how it's done. **And if you feel that you can implement some of the best practice in corporate responsibility but not follow all the way into the ethical debate, then we will still have achieved much of our purpose.**

One of the major reasons for being ethical – which merits discussion in much more depth than there is room for here – is that ethics are an excellent tool for predicting social issues that will affect organizations in the coming years. Many of the social changes which have affected companies in the last couple of decades have been preceded by intense ethical discussion. This discussion, though, was virtually ignored by business. People were talking about women's rights for some years before the women's movement developed, and with it the pressure which led to legislation which has profoundly affected companies' hiring policies.

Environmental issues have high been on the public agenda for over ten years now, and the Green movement is becoming a powerful political lobby. There are signs that stronger legislation is on its way; yet companies such as British Petroleum, British Gas, British Rail and Total Oil were still flouting the relatively weak Control of Pollution Act in 1988 according to newspaper reports. Obviously the government will be under pressure to tighten the Act, and the cost to the companies of complying with the revised laws is likely to be much higher than if they had obeyed previous legislation.

When society decides that things are going to have to change, there is a *cost* to bringing about that change. If business chooses to play no part in the debate about change, then it cannot complain if it is landed with the bill. The absent are always wrong. The reactive role is the loser's role.

The Lean Organization

One of the major social changes which is already happening is the hollowing out of the organization. When you look inside many companies now, especially in manufacturing, you find fewer people. We call a company like this a Lean Organization.

This sort of company seeks efficiency by moving functions outside of itself, where labour costs can be more closely monitored, control is retained by product specialists and production may be nearer the customer. The extreme example of this was when Firestone sold their radial tyre manufacturing operations to Japan's Bridgestone – only to buy the tyres back again to sell under Firestone's name.

The lean company comes complete with a whole new set of managerial challenges. The structure has changed. It is moving from being an **organization** to being an **organism**, a living creature, made up of parts which inter-relate. It is composed of networks, all of which contribute to the whole. Lines of authority no longer radiate only from the top, as they do in the structure of the conventional organization. The lines now go upwards and sideways as well as down.

The standard approaches to management all have in common that they are ways of running something. But the fundamental task in the lean company is a bringing together, a harmonizing and orchestrating of the network of outside organizations, organizations which a manager cannot be expected to 'run'.

A few years ago, managers and researchers in the United States set out to study corporations which had outstanding ethical and economic reputations. The common factor in their structure was that they were all networked organizations.

Twenty highly successful companies in the US and UK were studied. Three traits were identified which contributed to their success: fairness, personal responsibility, and purpose. These ethical elements were the cement which allowed the businesses to link together a large number of issues, and to organize themselves in a way which produced high profits.

We shall be demonstrating principles for high-ethics, high profit organizations. **High-ethics, low-profit organizations do not survive. High-profit, low-ethics organizations** *should* **not.**

It was found that the successful network organizations practised a tough-minded fairness in all their dealings. They were obsessively fair. They did not try to take unfair advantage of either their employees or their suppliers. They treated all their stakeholder groups alike.

Successful network organizations thus go out of their way to be fair. They also demand fair treatment in return. The idea of negotiating a wage deal which is fair, as opposed to one which is the minimum the management can get away with, may seem madness to many managers, but there is method in this madness. Whereas managing a corporate culture requires intensive hands-on management, fairness is self-managing. In a network organization you can't practise intensive hands-on management with all the groups which are crucial to your success.

Culture

Corporate culture is a popular concept: many books have been written about its importance in the success of a company. We oppose the view held commonly today in business circles that a strong culture is automatically a good thing. Ethics may be the heart of an organization's culture, but the myths, symbols, rituals and customs which go up to make that culture strangle it and destroy its vitality.

By its nature, a strong culture subjugates individual responsibility. That is the core of our objection to it: we believe that it places responsibility with the group, not with the individual. We shall return to this argument later.

Fairness

So how is this fair deal achieved? It is necessary to accept the limits of control possible within a network. Don't try to extend the range of control – an ethical company instead tries to establish an expectation of fairness. When managers can no longer ensure results through authority or control they must rely on agreements which are seen as fair by all parties.

Fairness is inherently *stable*. Authority and control are naturally unstable, because they rely on one party being more powerful than another. Authority and control therefore need hands-on management, but fairness manages itself. The emergence of the networked company forces managers to observe a standard of fair dealing with other stakeholder groups which should be the norm in all companies.

The second common trait found by the survey of successful companies was a commitment to *personal responsibility*. The trend in management today is towards functioning in groups or teams, and seeing responsibility in those terms. The responsibility lies in the operating units and in the companies themselves. But in successful networked companies responsibility is individual, rather than collective. The individual is assuming personal responsibility for the actions of the firm.

This brings us back to the paradox which is central to business ethics. How can you be responsible for something which is outside your control? To accept that this is possible means moving outside conventional thinking.

Virtually all academic research is labelled 'scientific'. The goal is to objectify and quantify – to follow predictable laws of the universe. We assume the potential predictability of everything – except, possibly, totally random events which may become predictable following new discoveries in quantum physics. Science tells us that object A cannot act on distant object B unless there is a connection between A and B. The individual A cannot affect B's individual responsibility without some connection between the two. That connection has traditionally been seen in terms of lines of authority or control. But we are talking about equals. So what is the connection?

The connection is the third factor which the researchers discovered: *purpose*. Shared purpose is what supports the network organization. The idea behind this is that each individual should know exactly *why* what they are doing makes sense on a day-to-day basis. One of the great lean corporations is IBM, which is emerging as a network organization.

For years IBM has been telling new employees that they are entering the world's best service organization. Their purpose is service. That purpose is not a goal – it is a way of operating, which drives each day's tasks. It binds IBM's network together, and it works because it provides a day-to-day reason for the various parts of the network to cooperate.

The bottom line on purpose is this: a network company is essentially a network which runs by mutual agreement. Purposes which are capable of supporting this agreement need to incorporate values which promote responsible behaviour. This responsibility extends both to the internal parts of the network and to the surrounding community which supports it.

These are new tools for new ways of working. If managers recognize that the hollowing out of companies requires new ways of managing, then the lean organization will indeed achieve high levels of performance. But the managers who fail to recognize that their company is rapidly becoming a network may find that the lean organization has no place for them.

The days of the networked organisation are here now, not in the future. Operating effectively within this structure means *all* the stakeholders must be considered. They all have different objectives. How can they be bound together?

The only way, we believe, is through a shared sense of purpose. The purpose itself need not be identical, but the different purposes must harmonize – they must be aligned with each other. And in order to have an alignment of purpose, there has to be agreement on the ground rules.

Ethics is all about ground rules: making sure that everyone is playing by the same rules, and that those rules are fair. Any attempt to align purposes while ignoring the ground rules, the ethics, just won't work.

That's enough theory for a while. Now we want to give you some practice.

CHAPTER TEN

THE ETHICS TEST

FIRST OF ALL check that you *do* know instinctively the difference between feeling good and feeling that you have done something wrong. When you have done something you are not comfortable about, do you....

	Yes	No
lose sleep?	——	——
smoke too much?	——	——
drink too much?	——	——
become irritable?	——	——
become suspicious?	——	——
find you can't relax?	——	——
feel afraid you'll be found out?	——	——
find you can't look people in the eye?	——	——
feel embarrassed with your family or friends?	——	——
find you get into rows over sports or politics?	——	——
need to go to confession, or to a counsellor?	——	——
keep going over possible consequences?	——	——
keep kicking yourself for having done it?	——	——
keep thinking of excuses and finding scapegoats?	——	——
..... or does it not bother you at all?	——	——

If you answered 'yes' to the last question, maybe this is the wrong book for you to be reading. But probably you will have answered 'yes' to several of the questions, and 'no' to the last. In other words, you have a pretty good idea of the difference, between things which make you feel good about yourself and things which you believe are wrong.

Now see how you feel about business.

	Yes	No
Do you believe that:		
it's a jungle out there?	——	——
most people in business cheat a little?	——	——
most business leaders are morally sound?	——	——
business doesn't need government regulation?	——	——
greed is what really motivates people?	——	——
greed is good?	——	——
because everybody does it, it's all right for me?	——	——

	Yes	No
Does your job:		
satisfy you?	——	——
make you feel you're doing something worthwhile?	——	——
ever make you feel cheap?	——	——
ever make you feel used?	——	——
ever make you feel distressed?	——	——
make you feel proud of yourself?	——	——
make you feel proud of your company?	——	——

	Yes	No
Have you ever, in a work situation:		
done something you consider seriously wrong?	——	——
felt pressured to do something seriously wrong?	——	——
considered doing something seriously wrong?	——	——
found a subordinate doing something seriously wrong?	——	——
found your boss doing something seriously wrong?	——	——

The answers to these questions should have started you thinking about your attitudes to right and wrong in your work life, and how they relate to your attitudes to right and wrong in your personal life.

Now, start thinking more carefully about the way you use terms like 'right' and 'wrong'. We use ethical language all the time. Listen to children talking – 'that's not fair!' is one of their commonest cries. Children have a strong preoccupation with fairness: it is one of their principal tools for making sense of what sometimes seems a nonsensical world.

Business people, too, make ethical judgments all the time – 'It's the wrong way to run the department, but we have to play by the same rules as the other departments'; 'It's not fair to say that we all have to meet our sales targets to get a rise, and then let Jim have it even though he didn't meet his, just because they play golf together'; 'What he did to get them to go along with that deal wasn't right, don't you agree?'

The words **'wrong'**, **'fair'** and **'right'** signal that these comments have an ethical content. Try this exercise: ask two work colleagues to join you. Get one of them to listen while the other two of you talk about a current work problem for five minutes. The listener should jot down every 'value' word which is said – 'good', 'bad', 'fair', 'unfair' and so on. We guarantee you'll be surprised how often ethical terms are used.

The more serious the work problem you chose to discuss, the more likely you are to have discussed ethical issues. It is the major happenings in life and business on which we make moral judgments – war, divorce, firing someone, resigning, or putting someone out of business. Given that we speak in ethical terms when we face major issues, we ought to know just what we mean by these terms.

For the next part of the exercise, pick out a few common ethical words from your vocabulary and write a brief definition, saying exactly what *you* mean by them and on what occasions *you* use them. Be simple and direct: write down just what you think.

What happens when people do this exercise is that they find it really difficult to write something that does not sound silly. They do not have a clear understanding of what they mean when they use ethical words. The sort of things they say are: 'It's against my principles'; 'It violates basic norms'; 'I wouldn't deal with anyone who did that.'

If you are saying this sort of thing, ask yourself: 'Why are *my* principles or *our* basic norms, as opposed to those of others, so important or right? And why does it matter who you would or would not do business with? Perhaps you don't like doing business with certain people or kinds of people. That doesn't mean there is anything wrong with those people or what they do.'

If you are doing this exercise with a few others – which we recommend – you may be starting to feel awkward. Don't – there are no right answers.

The point of the exercise is not to make anyone feel angry or embarrassed. It is to show that we need to pay attention to this part of our everyday thinking and speaking, especially when we are talking about major issues. The other important thing to note is that ethical talk is often critical – it is used to condemn someone or something that we do not agree with. If we say someone is unethical, we are serving notice that we think it is all right to be unethical back.

We are also usually looking for support in our judgment. When we make an ethical statement, it is often followed by 'don't you agree?' That is how *you* get ethical support to do something you don't feel so good about.

The last lesson to be learned from this exercise is that we use ethical talk to signal whether someone belongs – if they are part of the group or outside it. Anyone labelled unethical is not part of the group and so is fair game for members of the group, because its ground rules do not apply to them. This is not a comfortable way to look at the role of ethics – but it's a way they are often used, and we need to be aware of it so that we can deal with it.

Doing The Ethics Test was probably uncomfortable for you. We said it wouldn't be easy, but as we've also said before, knowledge is power. Utilising ethical tools to make difficult

**business decisions will give you power. It will give you a real
edge over your competitors – the ethics edge.**

Real problems

Now we shall look at ethics in relation to the sort of real
problems facing companies today.

1. Your company builds whatsits, the primary component of
which is the widget. For as long as you can remember, you have
bought your widgets from Old Sam, and you now buy 90% of
Old Sam's production. But now a big company has moved into
the widget business, and has offered to supply you at 20% less
than you have been paying Old Sam.
   *Is your standing relationship with Old Sam and his dependence on you
any consideration whatever? What do you do? Do you have any
obligation to Old Sam?*
2. You run the new product department at Company A. All
the companies in your sector are trying hard to develop a new
and more efficient thingummyjig. The research department has
just come up with a viable model and the engineering department is refining it for production. One of your major competitors, Company B, knowing that their research people cannot
develop a thingummyjig in a reasonable length of time offers
you a job in charge of their new product department at twice
your present salary. Your boss at Company A says he can't
possibly match that but does offer a rise of 20%, because he
values you.
   *Should you feel free to accept the competing offer from Company B? If
you do accept it, should you feel free to develop for Company B the
thingummyjig designed at Company A?*
3. A worker in a car factory becomes convinced that the
bonnet latch on the new model Seermobile is not secure enough,
and in a small number of cars may well pop open at high speeds,
probably causing an accident or, at the least, considerable
damage to the car itself. He goes to his supervisor and insists that

the latch be redesigned, but he is told that production is too far under way, the cost would be too great and the delay intolerable. He goes to the General Manager and gets the same reply.

Is the worker justified in going to the newspapers?

4. Your company sells pharmaceutical products in a developing country. One of them, Wellness Plus, promises to provide an effective cure for a common children's illness. But you find, much to your horror, that the product is being systematically misused, with sometimes serious medical consequences, by people who are mostly illiterate and have no medical supervision. At the same time, the product is selling like hot cakes and has brought your balance sheet back into the black. You've been able to postpone planned redundancies.

What do you do?

5. Your Fashion Jean Co. could save almost 30% on labour costs by moving from Sheffield to Sotogrande.

Should you move?

6. *Is it ever right to lie?*

7. Your factory is located in an inner city, with a local population which is mostly black and Asian. Only 9% of your work force is non-white, however, although most of the jobs can be learned in a matter of a few weeks.

Do you have an obligation to hire more black and Asian workers? Is it good business to do so?

8. You run a large textile company, but you are not making any money producing textiles. You fight and win large concessions from your work force. The shareholders are impatient for dividends. There's a juicy computer company up for grabs down the road.

What obligations have you to your workers, who have, in effect, given you the money with which you are considering your purchase? The concessions, needless to say, were aimed at keeping the company working and thus keeping their jobs.

Now try the Company Ethics Checklist.

	Yes	No
Is your company:		
friendly?	⎯	⎯
proud of its products or services?	⎯	⎯
comfortable and personal (even if it's big)?	⎯	⎯
anonymous and impersonal (even if it's small)?	⎯	⎯
proud of its reputation?	⎯	⎯
fearful?	⎯	⎯
fair in promotions, salaries, redundancies?	⎯	⎯

	Yes	No
Does your company:		
trust its employees?	⎯	⎯
have a company hero? who?	⎯	⎯
have a rigid and formal hierarchy?	⎯	⎯
encourage aggressiveness?	⎯	⎯
condone 'cut-throat' competition?	⎯	⎯
condone 'cutting corners'?	⎯	⎯

	Yes	No
Do you and your fellow employees:		
feel you're being watched all the time?	⎯	⎯
trust the company?	⎯	⎯
trust the competence of those at the top?	⎯	⎯
trust the honesty of those at the top?	⎯	⎯
trust the decisions made at the top?	⎯	⎯
trust the decisions made below you?	⎯	⎯
feel equal in dignity to those above you?	⎯	⎯
feel equal in dignity to those below you?	⎯	⎯
feel that ethics is an explicit concern at the top?	⎯	⎯
or among those around you?	⎯	⎯

Ethics as ground rules

A Chinese proverb says, 'The master knows the rules without suffering them; the servant suffers the rules without knowing them.'

A person's ethics are the basic ground rules by which he or she acts. We often give complex explanations of our actions, but in fact we act for simple reasons. These ground rules are a framework for defining which actions are personally permissible, and which are not.

In the same way, the ethics of an organization are the ground rules by which it acts. As we said before, this is not the definition of an organizational 'culture'. 'Culture' has become part of the standard lexicon of management, and many excellent, thoughtful managers believe that it is of fundamental importance.

We understand why talk of organizational culture has struck such a deep chord in managers. They sense that there is something correct about concern for meanings, symbols, myths, or whatever it is that constitutes a culture. This instinct is sound, but organizational culture is the wrong vehicle for such concern.

The common definition of culture is 'the way we do things around here'. It is about *how* things are done rather than *why*. It is essentially conservative: it judges the future by the past. Because it is rooted in tradition it reflects what *has* worked rather than what *will* work. A strong culture is predisposed not to change. The stronger the culture, the more resistant it is. But for a culture to persist, and to serve those who work and play in it, it must be able to learn and to profit from those lessons – in other words, to change.

The connection between culture and ethics is made when the organization is in crisis. If you want to change a culture, you *must* talk about ethics. Changing culture without ethics is like trying to change a flat tyre without a jack. The only change mechanism is through ethics, because only ethics ask *why* things are done.

Companies which have been in business since before the First World War have had to change to survive. A study in 1982 of New York Stock Exchange companies which have never missed a dividend in one hundred years found that not one of them was in the business it started in. And they are all high-ethics companies.

We are arguing for companies with weak culture and strong ethics. They are the companies which will be equipped to cope with the change demanded by other companies – or even by the opponents of business – who choose to draw up the lines of conflict on an ethical battleground.

How ground rules work

Motorola, a leading semiconductor and electronics firm, decided to infuse the whole company with the participatory management style which had proved very successful in several divisions. It met with a problem, the common syndrome: 'Although we're giving lots of pep talks and really trying in every way at every level, nothing is happening.'

When Motorola looked at the problem, they discovered that one of the company's ground rules was: 'All that really matters is the numbers.' This ground rule translated into management commitment to what could be measured in quarterly reviews, and nothing else. Once Motorola took note of this ground rule, it moved quickly to make the participation programme and the ground rule compatible – adjusting both in the process. If the ground rule had been ignored, Motorola would still be paying consultants to give pep talks in participation training programmes.

Sometimes the ground rules are outside the organization.

A leading overseas diesel engine manufacturer was worried about reports that the legislature was planning new tougher legislation on emission levels. The industry already felt over-policed. At a meeting to consider the problem, the PR people suggested a publicity campaign against the new regulations. The engineers complained that it wouldn't be technically possible to comply. The company lawyer proposed lobbying the politicians. But the Managing Director was thinking ethically.

He was taking all the stakeholder groups into account, and asking 'what is fair?' He wasn't asking 'what is the minimum we can get away with?'

He proposed that the company start to redesign its engines to stay ahead of the legislation, and lobby to have its proposed redesign incorporated into the legislation. He was looking at the ground rules of the public and of the legislature, and drawing the conclusion that the ground rules of his industry would be forced to shift. The public ground rule was: 'It's not fair that we should pay for pollution controls in our petrol engines while business doesn't have to with its diesel engines.' The legislature's ground rule was: 'If we want to stay in office, we can't be seen to favour big business at the expense of the public.'

This is a true story. Regulations almost identical to the company's redesign proposal passed after a tough legislative battle. The company was a year ahead of its competitors in getting products to market which complied with the regulations, and its share of the market increased dramatically. In fact, its next problem was that if it took too much of the market, people would think it had somehow rigged the regulations. *This company had found the ethics edge.*

Reverse Engineering

How do you discover exactly what the ethics of a person or a company are? The answer is, through the ground rules. But if you want to uncover the ground rules, don't ask, observe. Ethics are about what you do, not what you say. The same holds good for companies. If ABC plc brags about its concern for employee safety, it is trying to make a point about its ethics. Yet the fact that employees regularly end up in casualty because of unsafe conditions at the plant tells us the true story about the company's ethics.

To find the true ground rules of your company, we suggest that you use the technique of reverse engineering. Take a recent decision, and analyse it backwards. Ask what alternatives the company considered in arriving at the decision. Then ask what information it looked at with regard to these alternatives. How did the decision makers evaluate the alternatives and information to reach the decision? By asking these questions, you begin to uncover the company's ground rules.

A common example of true ground rules which conflict with expressed ground rules is found in the dilemma of many women managers who find that they can progress to senior middle management in their company, but no further. The company has a policy of equal opportunities, but one of the true ground rules is that no women should hold operating power. And if line management experience is also a ground rule requirement for promotion, then women don't get promoted.

Ground rules can pose other difficulties for female executives. For example, high-level male executives often operate on the ground rule: 'Take what you can or the other guy will take it.' But female executives often operate on the conflicting ground rule: 'If I always have to be trampling on somebody to get ahead, it's not worth it.' This conflict in ground rules puts the female at a considerable disadvantage.

The options available to her, in this example, are to change her male superiors' ground rules; to change her own ground rules; to accept the limitations imposed on her by her own ground rules – in other words, that she won't get the big promotions – or to leave the company, and find one where there is no ethics gap between her own ground rules and those of the company. That's how a lot of companies lose a lot of talent.

The Ethics Gap

We call the difference between your ground rules and your company's ground rules the Ethics Gap. It is important to know this gap – once you have identified it you can decide your strategy for dealing with it. Unless you are the owner-manager of a small business, there is bound to be a gap somewhere. So this is how to identify it:

Find your own ground rules
Make a list of the values that you think are most important for
you as a manager. Draw a line, and make a list of ways of doing
things as a manager in the way they you think they *should* be
done, and a second list of things you think managers should
never do.

Take these lists to work with you for a day or two, and make
some structured observations. Ask yourself: How often are the
things that I do motivated by the values on my list? How many of
my co-workers would identify these as my main values? When
do my actions exemplify ways I should act as a manager? How
often do I do things that I regard as unacceptable for a
manager?

Just make notes about all this. Don't try to evaluate your
behaviour at this stage. Be honest, as the information is strictly
private. You will know if you are being honest, because you will
come up with lots of things you're doing that you consider
unacceptable. The minimum number of unacceptables for most
managers is around a dozen per day.

Then identify your organization's ground rules
Repeat the first phase of the exercise, this time asking the
questions about your company rather than yourself. What does
your organization value? What ways of behaving does it reward
in managers? What ways of behaving does it consider unacceptable in managers? Take this list to work with you, and look
carefully at what you see going on around you. Pretend you are
a consultant hired to observe the ethics of your organization.

Once you have identified your ground rules and the ground
rules of your organisation, you can start to do some assessment.
Ask yourself: where are the largest gaps between my ground
rules and those of my organization? Where can I adapt? Where
can I not – or where should I not adapt? Are the differences
which can't be resolved important? Can I move the organization
in my direction on any of these points?

**Most people who do this exercise conclude that it is the
organization which is stopping them from being ethical. Of**

course they would act more ethically if only someone or something would let them. The question is, who is responsible for what happens in organizations?

This issue of responsibility, of the individual versus the organization, continues to be our basic theme. It is at the heart of many of the toughest management problems. Let us examine some more tools for solving these problems.

The problem of the commons

Sometimes everyone can be right, and sometimes they can all be wrong at the same time. In medieval times, herdsmen used to graze their cattle on common pasture – 'commons'. Each herdsman had the right to graze his herd on the commons, and the group shared the cost of maintaining the pasture – that is of keeping others off and protecting the cattle from wolves, etc.

This works as long as disease, war and natural calamities restricted the number of herdsmen and cattle. Then things improve — the war ends, a new clean water supply reduces disease. Each herdsman can add to his herd, and, being self-interested, wants to improve his standard of living. If he adds an animal, he receives the full benefit of it – the cost of feeding is small, since the cost of maintaining the common pasture is shared. Each herdsman's individual interest is served by adding to his herd as fast as he can. And the inevitable result is that the pasture becomes crowded and overgrazed.

Eventually the commons is destroyed, and everybody loses. Who is responsible? Everyone and no one. Each herdsman acted rationally and without ill will. The group made no decision. Group irresponsibility resulted as if by accident.

The problem of the commons is one of the prime difficulties in organizations today. When employees and managers see the organization as having a large pool of resources to which they all need access for their own purposes, the organization essentially becomes a commons. The overall performance of the organization becomes less important than the day-to-day battles everybody fights to improve their relative positions.

The real battle is usually fought over the budget. The budget is a hard measure of how much the firm values what we do. If we feel that what we do is important, it is rational for us to look for increased support for our function and increased pay for ourselves and our staff. More important, if we don't ask for more, we know we'll get less. The budget is a kind of commons because each of us approaches it rationally in an effort to get what we can for our department. Although we realize that overall this doesn't make sense, we assume that someone else somewhere will sort out a fair distribution. The responsibility is not ours.

But the people who we imagine will sort it out usually do not have the information to tell what is really needed down the line. At best, playing the game this way means that the budget process is a time-consuming mess. At worst, the budget commons is depleted.

If you want to find the critical problems affecting your organization, ask what commons exist in the organization. This is one of the key lessons that consideration of ethics teaches about management. Once you have identified the budget, common staff (researchers, for example), office space, non-budgeted office supplies and other obvious commons, keep thinking. You are likely to identify many of the critical problems which make your life difficult and your organization less profitable.

Justice

The next issue is justice. Dividing the pot up fairly is the toughest problem of all. Management and unions both feel that they have justice on their side, when they sit on different sides of the negotiating table. If everybody pursues their own definition of justice to the bitter end, there might be no pot left to divide.

We have said that the answer to the question 'who is responsible?' can often legitimately be answered 'no one'. If we are to help companies to work both ethically and effectively we need to bring responsibility back in. Responsibility is the only effective force, because it is the only one which can break through the conflicting gridlock of interests posed by the commons dilemma. We must *create* responsibility.

A foreign public telephone company wanted to increase its call charges. They argued that they needed the increase because labour costs had risen substantially. But they had just had an increase to cover the costs of modernizing equipment, and had not mentioned the labour costs then. The government felt that a line had to be drawn, and they drew it. No increase. Previously, the phone company had tried asking for permission to start charging for information calls, including directory enquiries. It was felt that this was sneaking an increase by the back door, so permission was refused.

Then one of the phone company's managers raised the question of justice. Labour costs were rising because some people couldn't be bothered to use the phone book. But this didn't apply to all customers – some were responsible, so why should they be penalized? The company launched a big advertising campaign aimed at discouraging irresponsible use of the operators' time. Then, dropping all arguments except that of justice, they went back to the government and asked again for permission to charge for information calls. They even offered to reduce basic rates slightly in return.

This argument was accepted, and they were allowed to charge for information calls. The revenues promptly increased to the level they would have reached with an overall increase.

If there are more responsible than irresponsible users of a commons, manage it by separating the interests of these groups.

But sometimes *all* the users are responsible, and other tools are necessary to find the just solution.

Best Result Ethics

What we call **Best Result Ethics** has had a variety of labels since philosophers first started to think about justice — hedonism, egoism, utilitarianism... but they all mean looking for the best result.

Best Result Ethics means: a person, organization or society should do what promotes the greatest balance of good over harm for everybody. Everybody? That means everybody significantly affected, which brings us back to stakeholder groups.

Ask yourself, 'Who has an identifiable stake in the outcome of this decision?' And ask, 'What is their interest?' It is not always easy to identify the stakeholder groups. Say you are looking at the issue of a company deciding whether or not to pay bribes in overseas markets. It's easy to identify the shareholders, the regulatory agencies, the company employees and managers, and foreign officials. But what about the citizens of the overseas country who must live with corrupt officials?

The first step in the best result decision process is to identify the significantly affected stakeholder groups. Then you have to choose the action which promotes the greatest balance of good over harm. That means there have to be alternatives available, but this is too vague to be helpful.

The second step in any complex decision is to identify the alternatives you believe to be most plausible. Then look at the alternatives that each stakeholder group would identify as plausible.

If you are dealing with a major problem, we advise you to get input directly from the stakeholder groups. Don't base your decision on what *you* think their plausible alternatives would be. Find out what is or is not acceptable, during the decision making process, not after you have committed substantial resources to a solution.

Then a decision has to be made. We know that to the manager, stakeholder groups are not created equal. Your responsibilities to each group differ. So the final step in the process is this: when you look at alternatives before you make the decision, assume that all stakeholder groups are created equal. But when you actually decide, prioritize the groups in terms of your responsibility towards each one.

How does this process differ from the traditional cost benefit analysis and risk benefit analysis? Surely these too are both based on Best Result Ethics? The answer is that cost benefit and risk benefit analysis do not distinguish between stakeholder groups; they give an answer irrespective of whether the relevant alternatives have been identified; and they inaccurately assume that assessment of benefits and costs is constant across stakeholder groups.

Best Result Ethics is a good ethical tool for the decision maker. The prescription is simple: start with the consequences. Begin by considering the consequences of what you do for those affected. Decision models are valuable more for the questions they pose than for the answers they generate.

Rule Ethics

Conflict is a fact of life in business, but not all conflicts are conflicts of interest. Many of the most difficult issues in business involve conflicts of rules rather than, or in addition to, conflicts of interest. We have already looked at the conflict of rules between an individual and an organisation. But what happens when rules differ between an organization and a society?

Rule Ethics means: a person or organization should do what is required by valid ethical principles; and a person or organization should not do anything contrary to valid ethical principles.

In other words, an action may be either obligatory or prohibited. If it is neither, it is permissible. You may do it, but don't have to. Rule Ethics is the simplest form of ethics, and also the oldest. The Ten Commandments are Rule Ethics. So is Marx's 'from each according to his ability, to each according to his need'. But the problem with Rule Ethics is that there are so many different sets of rules. One set of rules says that meat eating is wrong; another says that it is right. One set of rules says that you can only have one wife at a time; another says you can have four.

The other difficulty with Rule Ethics is that there are two kinds of rule: many, perhaps most, rules are not categorical. A categorical rule allows absolutely no exception. Prima facie rules, however, do.

A prima facie rule takes the form: *other things being equal,* one should tell the truth, obey the law, and so on. Even the law allows for prima facie rules. It is against the law to drive after drinking more than a certain amount of alcohol. But if you had had one glass of wine too many, and the person next to you started to haemorrhage and the only way to save their life was for you to drive them to hospital, the law would allow a plea of special circumstances.

If you had promised to sell a friend the rights to a patent, and then discovered he intended to sell it to a terrorist organization who were going to use it to develop a new form of explosives which could pass undetected through airport security checks, you would be ethically permitted – indeed obliged, in terms of Best Result Ethics – to break that promise.

This distinction is important. Very often, critics of business build what appears to be an excellent case against an organization's actions because they treat all rules as categorical. They say, for instance, that bribery is always wrong. It may often be wrong, but by taking the interests of all the stakeholder groups into account, an ethical case can be made for it.

Let us assume you are competing for a contract in a central African country where no contracts are ever awarded without bribes being received. Your Japanese and German competitors are prepared to pay the bribes; your products are as good as theirs, and your costs are competitive; four hundred people will be put out of work if your company doesn't get the order. No reasonable person could argue that the rule 'no bribery' does not at least merit a debate in this case – in other words, that it is a prima facie rule.

The issue of sanctions against South Africa is another where business may concede victory to its critics because it is unprepared to engage in ethical debate. We are neither advocating sanctions nor criticising them: we are simply pointing out that by identifying the different types of rules and adding the tool of Best Result Ethics a different solution may present itself.

Groups who act according to ideology rather than interest are seldom accurately anticipated by business. If you are dealing with the media, environmental groups or political bodies, knowing their ground rules will help you forecast how they will respond to your actions.

This is also vital in overseas markets. Learn the ground rules of the stakeholder groups in those markets by reverse engineering: look at what the firms who succeed in those markets do – and you will learn how to sell there too.

Best Result Ethics and Rule Ethics give you information with which to make your decision, but you still need to decide and act. There is one more type of ethics to consider.

Social Contract Ethics

A social contract is an implicit agreement about the basic principles, or ethics, of a group. Any organization is a web of implicit agreements, from the amount of time workers can spend in the toilets to the ability of the manager to make his staff work all weekend on an urgent project.

Contracts, both written and unwritten, govern all our lives. Social Contract Ethics provide a test of their soundness: a contract is sound if parties to the contract would enter the contract freely and fairly.

How can you tell if members of an organization would agree to their contracts freely and fairly? The thinking manager uses Social Contract Ethics to ask:

- Do I agree to this contract or do I just live with it?
- If I were the man who is working for me, would I accept this contract?
- If I were my boss, would I accept this contract?

If you were sitting on the other side of the table, would you think the deal you had reached was fair? This comes back to what we were saying about the network organization. Social Contract Ethics will hold it together.

This is the positive side of Social Contract Ethics. But there is a high price to pay for not recognizing these contracts and making sure they are fair. If you do not know the agreements by which your organization operates, it is difficult to institute significant changes. Significant changes in organizations generally shift the social contract for the parts of the organization which are not keen on the change. If the shift is not seen to be fair, they'll resist it. That resistance may not work, but it will certainly cost.

If you ignore the agreements, you will find it very hard to bring about change. Everyone who does not know whether they will be treated fairly will have a stake in resisting the change. On the other hand, if you make a clear commitment to fair agreements, radical change becomes a real possibility.

Purpose

These, therefore are all the ingredients of the ethical mix: stakeholder groups, ground rules, the 'commons', Best Result Ethics, Rule Ethics and Social Contract Ethics. What binds all these ingredients together to produce a high-ethics, high-profits business?

The answer is **purpose** – it's important to distinguish between goals and purpose. A goal is a target towards which one aims. When you've reached it, you need to set another one. A purpose, on the other hand, is a way of being or functioning which is seen as being valuable in itself.

The thinking manager, seeking to know the purpose of his company, asks:

- Why is the existence of this company worthwhile?
- Why should I and my co-workers do our job and pursue company goals with maximum commitment?

These are philosophical questions, but the need to ask them is real. Purpose gives a company a sense of who it is, where its goals come from, and why trying hard matters.

Purpose is the key which you add to all the information you have collected in the ethical approach to decision making. Follow your purpose, and you have your decision. Let it be the foundation, as an assurance that your decisions and actions collectively have meaning.

Once managers and employees accept the purpose of a company as worthwhile, they will assume individual responsibility. They will stop pointing fingers, and will solve 'commons' problems for themselves. They will think in the short term or long term as appropriate. They will manage and work purposefully.

We close this section with four principles for the high – ethics business:

- High-ethics organizations find it easy to work with diverse internal and external stakeholder groups. The ground rules of these organizations make the good of these stakeholder groups part of the organization's own good.
- High-ethics companies are obsessed with fairness. Their ground rules emphasize that the other person's interests count as much as their own.
- In high-ethics companies, responsibility is individual rather than collective, with individuals assuming personal responsibility for the actions of the business. These companies' ground rules say that individuals are responsible to themselves.
- The high-ethics organization sees its activities in terms of a purpose. This purpose is a way of operating that members of the organization value. And purpose ties the organization to its environment.

CHAPTER ELEVEN

DEVELOPING A CODE OF ETHICS

BEFORE YOU START to draw up a code of ethics there are two questions you must ask yourself:

- Does senior management accept that commitment to the code can only be brought about by encouraging every single member of the organization to participate in developing and implementing the code?
- Is senior management prepared to commit the resources necessary for this?

If you can't answer 'yes' to those two questions, don't waste your time. This is a harsh judgment, and a lot of people may disagree with us. But we feel strongly that half-baked ethics are worse than no ethics. If a small group of senior managers draws up a code which is then sent down by memo from the top, it will be filed where it belongs – in the waste paper bin. Remember social contract ethics. Senior management must practise what it preaches.

A company-wide training programme is essential, and the ethical code must also become a fundamental part of the induction process for new employees. No one should be exempt, from the postroom clerk to the new Marketing Director.

If you're prepared to do it properly, these are the steps to follow:

The Managing Director must be the driving force. It should be his or her task to draw up the outline code which will be the starting point for discussion.

The outline should cover three areas:

1 The purpose of the organization, and the values it wants to hold firm to while carrying out that purpose. This says what *kind* of organization you want to be.
2 Operating principles. This says *how* you are going to become that kind of organization.
3 Specific principles, and examples of what they mean in practice. This gives the detailed illustration of *what* to do in day-to-day situations.

One of the first values, of course, should be adherence to the spirit of the code. And an underlying theme of the specific principles should be that if something isn't clear, you ask for help.

When the MD has the outline, it should then be circulated to senior management. At this stage it should also be made public within the organization that the code is being developed, and general comments and suggestions invited.

A small group should be formed actually to write the code. It could have as few as three members, or a maximum of six. One of the members, however, should be the organization's legal advisor. It is useful if the others can come from different functions.

The group should incorporate the response from senior management and general views received, and present a revised and more detailed outline to the MD for review. When the MD's review has been added, this becomes the draft code.

Now the draft code should be circulated as widely as possible throughout the organization. The object is to get every member of staff feeling 'this is *our* code'. Feelings of ownership are the most potent way of ensuring that something is looked after, be it a code of ethics or a shiny new car.

Every comment made should be acknowledged and considered by the drafting group. If any individual item seems particularly controversial, it would be worth having a meeting to discuss it with the groups most concerned. The whole process will not take less than a month, and may well take three months

or more, depending on the size of the organization. But at the
end, you will have a code of ethics which fully reflects your
purpose and one to which your employees will be prepared to
commit themselves.

Implementing the code

You have taken care to draw up a code to which all your
employees will feel able to subscribe. Now they need to
understand how it works: the next section gives guidelines to
help to communicate the commitment throughout the
organization.

PART III

Communication

CHAPTER TWELVE

COMMUNICATING THE NEW STRATEGY

THIS IS A 'how to' guide which will work for communicating any strategy. It is slanted towards corporate responsibility and business ethics, but in fact it will work for anything you need to communicate through your organization.

So often we have read books – worthy books, even profound books – which have put the case for a particular business strategy or new approach to a business issue. And once they have explained it, they leave the reader to work out how to implement it. But any MD will tell you that it is not making decisions that is the problem: it is carrying the rest of the organization along with those decisions.

You might agree with everything we say. You might be prepared to tell your board that you want to make business ethics part of the way your company does business, but how do you let everybody else know?

This section is devoted to helping organizations to work through a communications strategy and programme. The quality of internal communications varies widely between organizations. Everybody knows that bad news is always communicated with the maximum efficiency – these proposals could help good news to spread as fast.

Start at the top

There has to be acceptance, enthusiasm and commitment at the very top of the organization before anything can be achieved.

This applies equally to an organization of a few people as to one with hundreds of thousands of employees. Leaders have got to lead.

We should also point out that communicating properly is time-consuming. Of course sending out memos and videos with instructions that they should be read and listened to is faster. But that is all wasted time – because the message will not get through. If you want the message to be not just received, but received, understood and acted upon, you must take time to do it properly.

Once the leader of the organization has decided he wants to get the commitment of the whole organization to corporate responsibility and business ethics, what happens next?

First and foremost, the senior management team must be enthused. Each individual must come to accept a personal commitment to corporate responsibility and the ethical approach. It is necessary to give sufficient time for individual members of the senior management team to voice any objections or concerns they may have. Those objections or concerns then need an adequate response from the leader whose idea it is.

Now you have the commitment of the senior management team. They understand the issue, they can see the benefits for the company, and they want to do something about it. Where do we go from here?

It is an important question, because to find out where we go to from here, the first thing we have to do is find out where 'here' is. In other words, generally speaking, after proper discussion senior managers can agree on where they want to get to. They are going on a route from A to B, and they are usually pretty good at defining B. After all, this is one of the best parts of being a senior manager – having the opportunity to set the objectives and goals of the organization.

But, as many companies have found to their chagrin, there is often no clear understanding of the dimensions of A. Even an organization which has been in business for a fairly short period of time will have a specific 'culture'. It is not a blank sheet of paper, and you need to be aware of what you are changing *from* as well as what you are changing *to*. Businesses need to apply significant resources to establish where they are at present – in other words, you need a full definition of A before you set off on the march to B.

If you don't know where you are going you are liable to end up somewhere else, and if you don't know where you are starting from you'll have difficulty finding the right path.

Find out where you're starting from

You need to know where you are before you set out. You also need to know what you are and who you are. How do you arrive at a definition of your current dimensions? In the Ethics Test, we suggested you pretend you were a consultant hired to evaluate the current state of your company's ethics. If you did that, you will have discovered that it is not an easy thing to quantify. It is very difficult for an insider to look at their company with an entirely open mind.

You need to examine the company ethos in detail, to find which ethical considerations currently operate in the business, using your own staff and/or external consultants. It is unlikely that insiders will be truly effective without the support of people expert in this field.

One of the key areas often overlooked in such audits or reviews is the attitudes, opinions and ethics of the middle management group. So often, in their view, they are expected to support the latest 'flavour of the month' coming from top management. Ironically, and sadly in many cases, though their views are usually consulted, their recommendations are not given full consideration. Yet this is the very group whose response, or lack of it, will condition the success of a survey and the ability of an organization to implement any strategy.

The survey will define A – where you are now, why you are there, what you are and how you got there. It will also, if it has been done properly, have determined how strong the culture of the organization is. It will talk to the strength of the culture and will indicate the purpose of the organization as it is understood by the different levels of employees within it.

How do you get from A to B?

We have discussed at length the importance of the purpose of the organization. We could also define point A as the present understanding of that purpose, and point B as the future understanding of that purpose.

If we accept that definition, then the path from A to B can be seen as the process of imbuing the whole of the organization with that sense of purpose. And on a regular basis, we need to assess how well the purpose is continuing to be understood and acted upon. **Communication is not a finite goal. It must be a continuing process, and it must have checks and audit points built in to ensure that it remains effective.**

The survey should have encouraged many people to develop an awareness of a sense of purpose. The process of developing a code of ethics should have helped to involve all the interested parties. So now there is an agreed purpose and code of ethics, and/or a commitment to corporate responsibility.

We cannot emphasize too strongly how important the role of the Managing Director is in underlining the commitment of the organization. The more seriously the MD takes the code, the more seriously everyone else will take it. A useful approach is for the MD to make a video discussing the code and its importance: this can be used as an introduction to training sessions and for induction purposes.

The Managing Director should now, ideally, talk directly to every member of his organization. If this is impracticable because of the size of the organization, then he must at least meet with as many levels of management as possible. Then the video could be used as an introduction to discussions further down the chain. It is of crucial importance firstly to communicate the MD's commitment, and secondly, to make sure that this commitment is properly articulated and supported by each individual manager when talking to his or her work group.

Survey after communications survey indicates categorically that the most important communications channel, and the one given highest status and priority by individual employees, is the one from a manager or supervisor direct to their staff.

We beg you to avoid at all costs the 'head office syndrome' scenario. You know the one. A manager and his ten or twelve staff sit round a video recorder. The manager says: 'Here's the latest important announcement from the lads at Head Office. It lasts fifteen minutes – I want you to watch it carefully – and then you can all get back and get on with the job.' This statement is usually greeted with a variety of responses from guffaws to titters, with cries of 'who's got the ciggies?' and 'mine's black, no sugar'. The video ends, and is often followed with a half-hearted plea from the boss for total coöperation and commitment... and from the audience, a repeat of the guffaws and titters, followed by 'where are the ashtrays?'

We believe that gaining commitment to a new purpose for an organization is a message of such fundamental importance it should not be left to an impersonal video, however professionally produced.

If the numbers are such that the MD has to talk to employees in very large groups, he should take care to have a meeting in advance with the managers. He should take the time to listen to them sincerely, and respond, at length if necessary, to their concerns. It may take a long time and we know that there are other important matters to be taken care of, but the feedback alone will be of inestimable value.

However it is done, the programme must ensure that managers at all levels have a full commitment to, and understanding of, the role which they can play. This is why we recommend a thoroughgoing business ethics training programme.

A code of ethics is best implemented by a rigorous training programme involving everyone from board level down to shop floor workers. At board level it could be done by informal presentation, in a briefing session; below board level we recommend a more formal approach. The training should be practically grounded and sessions should be participatory, rather than a series of lectures. It can't be done in less than a day, or with groups of more than thirty people. The approach should be at least as professional as in any other training your organization provides.

Once your managers have been trained, the ideal is for them to train their own staff. This reinforces the value of the training for the group whose commitment is essential for the success of the code. Some managers, however, may be uncomfortable delivering a programme on ethics: they could receive additional specific training on carrying out the training themselves, and complete support materials would need to be provided.

The other approach is to use outside trainers to train directly at all levels, or to train your own in-house trainers to deliver this programme. This has the advantage that all members of your organization are seen to be learning together, rather than some 'telling' others how to be ethical. Care would have to be taken that the trainers had sufficient background to discuss knowledgeably the issues that really matter in *your* organization. The training should be done over as short a time as possible. Here again, the MD needs to state very publicly the priority which he gives to attendance at the training sessions.

The training must also become part of the induction process for new employees. We recognize that these prescriptions are not easy, and will demand considerable resources. Otherwise, however, the code will remain only a piece of paper to which people may or may not pay lip service. This way, you will be building an organization which can face the twenty-first century with confidence.

Beyond quality

This sort of training programme would be the ideal. But whatever you do, the message that needs to be communicated is that

corporate responsibility = individual responsibility

There has been a proliferation of quality programmes of late, preaching the message of quality, defined by some experts as conformance to requirements. This says that it is better and cheaper to have a high-quality organization which does not generate faults than a low-quality organization which fixes faults as they arise. Most quality programmes try to define the cost of quality by establishing the costs of the lack of quality.

This philosophy also holds that everyone in the organization is responsible for quality. In other words,

$$\text{individual quality} = \text{corporate quality}$$

Hardly anybody has difficulty with this concept. Furthermore, companies rarely have difficulty coming to terms with the necessity for all parts of the organization to accept the need for quality.

Quality philosophy asks what happens when customers are unhappy with the product. We all know the rule of thumb: a happy customer may tell one other person, but the unhappy customer will tell ten other people. Likewise, organizations have no difficulty telling staff that even if you do not deal directly with external customers you certainly deal with your fellow employees, with internal customers who can be greatly affected by low-quality service.

Companies are happy to spend hours, days, even months communicating the importance of quality to their staff. But even more fundamental than quality is responsibility. You are responsible not just for quality in what you do. You are also responsible for the whole business.

In some cultures this would not be regarded as a revolutionary statement. But the reverse side of this individual responsibility is the second equation:

$$\text{individual responsibility} = \text{corporate responsibility}$$

The company has a responsibility to each individual, and its decisions ought to embrace individual needs. Each individual needs to make decisions as if he were running the business, and the business needs to make decisions which will take into account each individual's issues and priorities. The extension of this argument is that the philosophy we are proposing is in every sense an enabling one. It says that because an individual is responsible, then that individual has value and is therefore empowered.

If you are reading this book and feeling that it's about as relevant to you in your organization as strawberries in January, take heart. What we are saying is that even if you feel your organization wouldn't know a socially responsible act if it hit it in the solar plexus, *you can make a difference.*

Your individual way of behaving does matter. You can be responsible. You can be ethical, even if those around you seem not to care. Because you have value as an individual, you can express that value and self worth through your sense of responsibility. We do not want to create a nation of Pollyannas, nor do we expect you to put your job on the line ten times a day. But we do believe that people learn by example, and if you as, say, a middle manager set an example of good practice and responsible behaviour, others will respond.

We really believe that people want to be good. If you give them an option, if you allow them to behave responsibly without feeling their job or promotion is on the line, they will do it. And you will all reap all the benefits, for yourselves and the company, that we have been discussing.

Whistle-blowing

We don't necessarily expect you to put your job on the line. But occasionally, once in every few careers, an issue comes up for which you might want to do just that.

Whistle-blowing gets an inordinate amount of publicity, because so much of the 'business ethics' literature is concerned with wrongdoing in business. You will have gathered that this is not our approach: we want to encourage people to do right, not to be forever pointing the finger at people who do wrong. But when it happens, almost invariably someone loses their job and hits the headlines at the same time. What do you do if you see your organization doing something wrong? What *should* you do? After all, we have just said that you are responsible for the entire business – not just the area where your job responsibilities lie.

The costs of whistle-blowing can be heavy. Charles Robertson, the Chief Accountant of Guardian Royal Exchange, was reportedly sacked for being too open with the Inland Revenue – a decision which could cost GRE up to £10 million in back taxes. Previously, he had disclosed that the company had avoided paying £1.6 million in taxes on an Australian deal. Then he sought assurances from the company that there were no other irregularities – but was eventually sacked. An industrial tribunal ruled he should have his job back, but the company refused to re-employ him. They paid him compensation of £91,000, equivalent to about two years' salary, but as he says: 'No one wants to take me on after the trouble with GRE. The compensation is grossly inadequate compared with what I lost because of my honesty. This must discourage other employees faced with an ethical dilemma from having the moral strength to do the right thing.'

An American whistle-blowing case had a better outcome for the whistle-blower, but while it was going on lives were lost. Dan Gellert was a pilot for Eastern Airlines with twenty-five years' experience. During flight simulation trials in 1972, he realized there was a possibly fatal defect in the Lockheed L-1011. The automatic pilot sometimes disengaged without warning ninety seconds before landing, at the most critical part of the approach. Dan Gellert raised the matter inside the company, but was not listened to. He reported the defects to the National Transportation Safety Board, but at the end of 1972 an Eastern L-1011 crashed, killing 103 people. Gellert pushed his report to the top of the company. It was ignored. A year later, another L-1011 which he was piloting nearly crashed and he went back to the NTSB.

This time the company demoted him, then grounded him. His ability to fly was questioned. He went through grievance procedures for seven months, then sued. He won *more* than he sued for ($1.6 million) as an expression of indignation by the judge. He is now a celebrated whistle-blower. He insists he never intended or wanted to be one, but 'couldn't do anything else'.

We can't offer easy answers to the individual. You will know if you have to blow the whistle. You will obviously start off by making your concerns known to your managers, then to the board. You may be able to resolve this Ethics Gap by leaving the organization. Or you may have to blow the whistle.

But we *can* offer answers to the company. What should a company's attitude be to whistle-blowers? Firstly it should listen to them, and secondly it should respond. But more important than either of these is that a company should make sure that the conditions for whistle-blowing never arise.

It should have free and open channels of communication. The whistle-blowing discussion underpins our thesis that weak culture and strong ethics should be the goal. An organization with a weak culture is open and accessible to those who have a contrary opinion: it will examine other views carefully and thoughtfully and, if appropriate, will adopt them. Conversely, organizations with a strong culture seek to suppress unwelcome views and opinions. They are therefore generally unprepared for corporate tragedy when it occurs.

Deeds, not words

Whether you go all the way with a company training programme or not, what is absolutely crucial in ethics is that you will be judged by deeds, not words. That is how it should be. There is no point producing a wonderful code of ethics and then acting contrary to it. If that were to happen ethics would surely be seen as yet another flavour of the month. Regardless of the size of the organization, and of where you as an individual are within the organization, acting ethically and responsibly brings its own rewards.

Getting everyone involved

We have digressed a little from the theme of how to communicate your commitment, but it was a necessary digression, because we needed to explain the importance of the two equations, how corporate and individual responsibility are the same thing.

Once a company has agreed its priorities for a corporate responsibility programme, it needs to communicate the reasons for these strategies clearly and succinctly. It should seek to empower each member of the organization by explaining the value of these strategies both to the organization and to individual members.

More importantly, the company should involve all the employees directly in the implementation of its strategies. It should give recognition to everyone who gets involved. Some ways to do this are:

- **Community service awards. These can be given both for quality and quantity of service**
- **Chairman or Managing Director's recognition of community relations activities – a company celebration, or a visit to any community organization where employees have won community service awards**
- **Encouraging partnerships**
- **Publicizing the activities of those who participate**

So often recognition for these activities stops at the top: the Chairman planting a tree; the Managing Director shaking the hand of the royal family. But very often there are hundreds of unsung employees in the lower levels of your organization, quietly implementing our principles about bridging the divide between life and work, contributing thousands of unpaid hours to the community.

There are any number of channels which you can choose for these communications. These may include:

- **The company newspaper**
- **The electronic mail noticeboard**

- **Management information letters**
- **Videos, where appropriate**

But the primary channel to use is that of example. Organizations should avoid being ensnared by the panoply of communications channels now available, because all of these speak to a strong culture. They should prefer to speak through their actions – and these actions will publicize themselves most effectively. Remember the best communication channel of all – the one from manager to staff. Target the managers and supervisors: their actions are the key.

Good news vs bad news

There is a problem with communications. When people say they want good communications, what they mean is they want to communicate the good news. Few people look for good communications channels for bad news. **Companies spend huge resources and energy on communicating the good news. When an audit is done, it is often discovered that the bad news is communicated twice as fast – even though there are no official channels for the bad news and no one was asked to communicate it.**

Why does this happen? How *does* everybody know so fast that the finance director has disappeared to Rio with that handsome young man from accounts? The thing about informal channels, or bad news channels, is of course that they are very rarely undistorted. The bad news is always embellished and adorned. The bigger the company, the more its faults are magnified and its virtues minimized.

Good news is rarely embellished and adorned – if anything, there is a tendency to play it down. A lot of the time this is because of the credibility gap. When anyone hears a message, the first thing they do is assess the credibility of the source. Depending on that credibility, they will then place a value on the message. So if the source is acting irresponsibly, that in itself sets up a communications culture which cannot be modified overnight.

Actions speak louder than words. It is better to show people than to tell them. The returns will follow.

Going public on your ethical code

When a company places ethics at the core of what it does, it should publicize the fact. Not just with its employees – we have already discussed how to do that – but with all its stakeholder groups. It also has a responsibility to encourage other companies to do the same, because we all know it only takes one rotten apple to spoil the barrel. You start in your own company, but you need to share the commitment. Other businesses are one of the principal stakeholder groups in this context. How can you publicize your commitment?

- **Encourage other companies to devote resources to ethical considerations.**
- **Take part yourself in debate on social change, and encourage other companies to take part as well.**

We all know that information technology and biotechnology will have an enormous impact on the development of business in the next decade and the next century respectively. The ethics of these issues have not been fully debated, and we fear that one major tragedy in either of these areas could bring such developments to a halt. Only the ethical approach can enable business to prepare itself for these tragedies. We have not discussed these areas, because they are the subject of a book in themselves. But the tools we have given are the tools which need to be applied.

Companies need to join the debate right now – not just on the best way to use information technology and biotechnology, but on the whys and wherefores of their place in society.

- Sponsor a conference to examine such issues along with government and community organizations.
- Publicize the results of that conference.
- Make use of corporate communications to underscore your commitment to the debate.

Your other stakeholder groups include your shareholders, your suppliers, your customers and your pensioners.

■ Your shareholders deserve more information, not less. Give them the maximum.

■ Work out new common ethical ground rules with your suppliers. Look at how much you buy from them and how you pay them: when you offer a new fair deal make sure you demand fairness in return.

■ Have a specific ethical code for your dealings with your customers. Make sure your sales force is trained to point out that one of the benefits of your product or service is the fact that it comes from an ethical supplier.

■ When you consider the investment of your company pension funds, make sure your fund managers consider the ethical implications of their investment strategies.

Politicians and state employees are another stakeholder group in this context. The government is obviously part of the community. You need to contribute to the legislative process. Then when the debate takes place, yours will be one of the voices sharing in the decision-making processes, and you will not be dismissed as simply responding out of self-interest.

■ Develop a close relationship with your local politicians. Many MPs and councillors have no experience of business. Invite them in to your company. Set up regular meetings.

■ Join the Industry and Parliament Trust, and offer Industrial Study Fellowships to Members of Parliament. These are informal attachments of an MP, MEP or peer to a company to give both sides greater understanding of how the other works.

■ Try setting up a similar organization at local level.

■ Encourage cross-exchange between your employees and civil servants. And do this at the lower levels of the organization, not just at the top.

■ Send out regular briefings to local councillors, civil servants and politicians – or perhaps a copy of the company newspaper.

These are just some of the channels open to you. We leave it to you to think of others particularly appropriate to your organisation.

CHAPTER THIRTEEN

CONCLUSION

AT THE BEGINNING of this book, we asked a number of questions. The most important was this one: Do you, as a business man or woman, want to feel good about yourself?

We have assumed that your answer was yes, and the rest of this book has been given over to offering you ways to help you to achieve that. We want you to feel proud to say that you're in business. And we hope that even if you do not feel completely proud at present, you can see how you can help build a company you can be proud of, at whatever level you operate and whatever size of business you are part of.

We also pointed out that businessmen are not bogeymen. And we hope that whether you are reading this as a business person or as a member of one of the groups traditionally hostile to business you will now accept this premise. Of course there are some wicked businessmen, just as there are some wicked doctors or wicked teachers or wicked politicians. But the vast majority are honest decent people who happen to make their living in business.

The problem is not with business people. As we have tried to demonstrate, it lies within the structures of business and the way it organizes its affairs. But if business is about anything, it is about exchanges and interchanges between people.

It is time to stop feeling helpless, and to see that there are ways in which you can bring together the kind of citizen you want to be in your private life and the kind of citizen you want your company to be in its public life.

Ethics play a central role in business, whether that role is recognized or not. A review of ethical considerations will bring enormous benefit to your business. We have sought to show that business ethics are *not* a contradiction in terms, but in fact are at the heart of all business activities.

We have put forward three arguments which could be seen as revolutionary in the context of current management thinking.

The first is that a strong culture is not necessarily a good thing. We have argued for a weak culture, with strong ethics. We have done this on two grounds – that a strong culture limits individual responsibility, and that it is by its nature opposed to change.

We have also posed the paradox that corporate responsibility equals individual responsibility. Nobody has tackled this paradox effectively. The conventional view of corporate responsibility is shown in the following common scenario.

The board has heard discussions on the problem of the inner cities. This company has only a marginal involvement with the inner cities, but the Chairman has been to dinner at Number Ten, where it was made clear that some action would be appreciated. As a result, the personnel director has been told to get on with 'it'. She in turn gives the job to a junior member of staff – someone who has just joined or is perhaps just about to retire. This man, knowing little about the subject, recommends talking to an organization which advises joining the local Enterprise Trust. (This is not to belittle enterprise trusts, which do an excellent job, but to point up the lack of lateral thinking in the conventional approach.)

The result of all this is that the Chairman sees the advantage of killing many birds with one stone. He attends meetings with other Chairmen. He gets to rub shoulders with royalty on a regular basis. He makes a modest financial contribution, which is seen as 'charitable'. The company gets some good PR.

Obviously this is the cynic's version of the way things are done, but in some cases, it may be uncomfortably close to the truth. It is great for the company, but does not do all that much for the community.

Our argument is that, where responsibility is concerned,

corporate = individual = corporate

and to bring about change this paradox has to be worked at.

Our third thesis is that business ethics is the key, and is fundamental to business success. It has not been easy to find large numbers of illustrations of the benefits of the ethical approach. It is more feasible to use the same tools as those which enable the cost of quality to be worked out, and examine the cost of a lack of ethics. We could, for instance, point to Distillers, which, after the way it handled the thalidomide affair, found itself with no sympathy or public constituency when the predatory Guinness came along. McNeil Laboratories, on the other hand, handled the Tylenol catastrophe by immediately wiping the shelves of the product, even though they were 99.9% certain that they had contained the problem. They recovered extremely well from their disaster.

There is a current fad of crisis management in public relations. PR companies advertise that they will help you work through any crisis. They offer to help you limit the damage. Business ethics do not seek to help you limit the damage; they seek to avoid the crisis in the first place. Increasingly, with the growth of technologies of all kinds, crises are tragedies and will not respond to a quick-fix solution.

The easiest way to avoid a corporate tragedy is not a strong culture and a slick PR company. It is a weak culture and an open communications system. Corporate tragedies rarely happen unannounced: often several people, or even scores of people, see it coming but are discouraged by a strong culture from drawing attention to the problem. The result can be a corporate tragedy of such massive implications that no amount of crisis management can bring it under control.

The manifestation of an organization's ethical approach is through corporate responsibility. It has to be central to its strategy, and the best way to make it central is to put business ethics at the core of everything the organization does. Corporate responsibility will never attain a central position in strategy without the moral case being made.

We are not dodging the issue of the bottom line. Business people rightly want to know how something affects the bottom line, and we agree that it is vitally important. Both corporate responsibility programmes and an ethical approach to business are aimed at profit. We have said nothing which is not intended to produce an improvement in your bottom line. We are not advocating altruism.

What we will say is that the lack of business ethics can ruin a career faster than anything else. And we can extrapolate from that statement even more certainly to say that lack of ethics can ruin a company faster than anything else. Everything we propose is aimed at enhancing performance. We see limited value in altruism for its own sake, but enormous value in responding effectively to community issues. In essence, our final equation is this:

corporate responsibility = individual responsibility = added value for the individual and for the company

We would not seek to underestimate the difficulties in applying the revolutionary concepts outlined in this book. That said, we have tried to indicate how individual managers or employees can act in a manner consistent with an ethical approach.

It would also be fair to say that we have by no means exhausted the subject of business ethics. What we have attempted to do, by making it the 'meat' in the sandwich as we outlined in the preface, is to accord it its rightful place as central to all the other considerations and to explain its ramifications in some detail.

In saying that, however, we are acutely aware that to do it full justice would take much more space than we have here. None the less, we see a value in raising the awareness and profile of business ethics, and over the course of the coming years we shall be actively engaging and encouraging the attention of companies in this subject.

EXCUSES WE HAVE KNOWN

IF YOU'VE GOT this far in the book, your persistence deserves a reward. So we'd like to share with you some of the excuses we have encountered for not incorporating corporate responsibility programmes. They don't necessarily come in this order, and often we get more than one at a time.

- **We have enough complications already**
- **This needs more study**
- **It's not our policy**
- **It's already our policy**
- **Too much paperwork**
- **In principle I agree, but...**
- **It's not in the budget**
- **It's really a matter of opinion**
- **It's probably too expensive**
- **We've always done it that way**
- **They don't care**
- **They won't do anything about it anyway**
- **There are no clear answers**

If you come across any more good ones, please share them with us. We can be reached at The Centre for Corporate Responsibility and Business Ethics, Strathclyde Business School, Glasgow G4 0GE.

BIBLIOGRAPHY

Anthony, W.P., et al (eds), *The Social Responsibility of Business.* Morristown, New Jersey: D.H. Mark Publication of General Learning Press, 1973

Baumhart, R.S.J., *Ethics in Business.* New York: Holt, Rinehart & Wilson, 1968

Behrman, J.N., *Discourses on Ethics and Business.* Cambridge, Mass: Oelgeschlager, Gunn & Hair, 1981

Blanchard, K. and Peale, N.V., *The Power of Ethical Management.* London: Heinemann Kingswood, 1988

Bowie, N., *Business Ethics.* Englewood Cliffs, New Jersey: Prentice Hall, 1982

Cook, R.A. and Ryan, L.V., 'The Relevance of Ethics to Management Education', *Journal of Management Development,* 7, 2, 28-32

Deal, T. and Kennedy, A., *Corporate Cultures.* Addison-Wesley, 1982

De George et al (eds), *Ethics, Free Enterprise and Public Policy: Original Essays on Moral Issues in Business.* New York: Oxford University Press, 1978

Goyder, G., *The Just Enterprise.* London: André Deutsch, 1987

Harvard Business Review: Ethics for Executives Series, President and Fellows of Harvard College, 1955

Pastin, M., *Hard Problems of Management.* San Francisco – London: Jossey Bass, 1986

Pastin, M., 'What to do about Ethics', *Chief Executive Magazine,* No. 46, Jul/Aug 1988

Pastin, M., 'The Hollow Corporation', *Executive Excellence,* Institute for Principle Centered Leadership, 1988

Solomon, R. C. and Hanson, K., *It's Good Business.* Atheneum Publishers, 1985

Srivastra, S and Associates, *Executive Integrity.* San Francisco – London: Jossey Bass, 1988

Velasquez, M. G., *Business Ethics.* Englewood Cliffs, New Jersey: Prentice Hall, 1982

INDEX